DATE DUE		

—Diseases and People—

TUBERCULOSIS

Alvin, Virginia, and Robert Silverstein

ENSLOW PUBLISHERS, INC.

44 Fadem Road   P.O. Box 38
Box 699   Aldershot
Springfield, N.J. 07081   Hants GU12 6BP
U.S.A.   U.K.

Library of Congress Cataloging-in-Publication Data

Silverstein, Alvin.
    Tuberculosis / Alvin, Virginia, and Robert Silverstein.
        p.   cm.
    Includes bibliographical references and index.
    ISBN 0-89490-462-0
    1. Tuberculosis—Popular works. I. Silverstein, Virginia B.
    II. Silverstein, Robert A. III. Title.
    RC311.S59 1994
    616.9'95—dc20   93-4686
                                                                CIP
                                                                AC

Printed in the United States of America

10 9 8 7 6 5 4

Illustration Credits:
American Lung Association, pp. 17, 48, 60; Florida TB-RD Association, p. 58;
©Institute for Tuberculosis Research, University of Illinois at Chicago, p. 37;
National Jewish Center for Immunology and Respiratory Medicine in Denver, pp.
18, 69, 71, 102; *The New York Times,* pp. 6, 30, 80, 86, 95; Office of Cancer
Communications, National Cancer Institute, Bethesda, Md., p. 43;
UPI/Bettmann, pp. 51, 83; William R. Jacobs / ©Howard Hughes Medical
Institute Research in Progress 1991, p. 99.

Cover Illustration: © John Michael/International Stock

Contents

Acknowledgments

The authors would like to thank Dr. Irwin Berlin of the American Lung Association for his careful reading of the manuscript and his many insightful comments and helpful suggestions.

Thanks also to Angelique Davis of the National Jewish Center for Immunology and Respiratory Medicine and Ruth K. Kasloff of the American Lung Association for their help in gathering illustrations for the book.

TUBERCULOSIS

What is it? An infectious disease caused by a bacterium; most commonly affects the lungs

Who gets it? All ages, all races, both sexes

How do you get it? Mainly by breathing air containing bacteria-contaminated droplets

What are the symptoms? Tiredness, lack of energy, weight loss, fever, night sweats, persistent cough, chest pain, blood in sputum

How is it treated? With antibiotics such as isoniazid (INH), rifampin, streptomycin, and PAS (para-aminosalicylic acid); curing TB may take nine months or more of continuous treatment; failure to complete treatment may result in TB becoming drug-resistant

How can it be prevented? Avoiding close contact with patients with active TB in poorly ventilated rooms; regular exercise, adequate sleep, and a good diet (including vitamins A, C, and E and the minerals zinc and selenium) may help strengthen the body's defenses against developing active TB. BCG vaccine is used in most of the world, with varying effect; not used in the United States

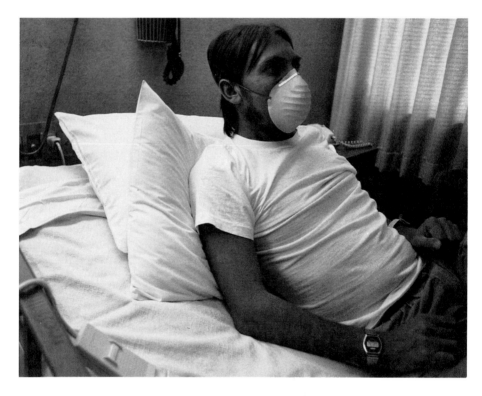

Tuberculosis is once again a disease on the rise in the United States. This patient had been fighting drug-resistant TB for eighteen months.

1

Return of the White Plague?

ecently a young couple in Westchester County, New
York, received some news from their doctor that
changed their lives dramatically. Their four-month-
old baby had been wheezing from a cold that kept hanging
on. At first the doctors suspected cystic fibrosis, a serious hereditary disease. Instead, tests revealed that the baby had
tuberculosis—and, in fact, his twin brother and his mother
also had TB. The babies' father and their five-year-old brother
did not have the disease, but they, too, had been infected by
the TB germ. Now the mother and her babies faced long
months of taking drugs to treat the disease. "I felt so immune," said the astonished mother, who commutes to
Manhattan for her work as a lawyer. "We live in this tiny

7

town in Westchester, in the middle of the forest. My kids never come into the city. We were totally floored."[1]

Actually, though the numbers of cases in suburban and rural areas are growing, the Westchester family is not typical of most TB patients today. Health workers are more likely to deal with people like Vincent, a Vietnam veteran who grew up in housing projects in New York and became a heroin addict; or Theresa, a woman with eight children who lives in a welfare-supported two-room apartment in Newark, New Jersey; or Debra, a former nursing assistant who became infected while nursing her sister and can no longer work because the current drugs cannot keep her strain of TB under control.[2]

Tuberculosis, commonly known as TB, has been a deadly threat for thousands of years. This disease, which mainly affects the lungs, killed so many people during the Middle Ages that it was called the White Plague. TB has also been known as *consumption* because it causes the body to gradually waste away and be "consumed."

Yet by the 1970s and 1980s most Americans had nearly forgotten about TB. In the United States and other industrialized nations, better living conditions and improved methods of prevention, diagnosis, and treatment had greatly reduced the number of people who got tuberculosis and the number who died from it. In fact, many doctors thought tuberculosis would be completely wiped out in the near future.

In the rest of the world, though, TB never really went

away. It is still one of the world's biggest killers, especially in the developing countries. Twenty million people suffer from the disease,[3] and each year nearly three million people die from TB—more than from any other infectious disease.[4] About one-third of the entire world's population is carrying the germ that cases TB,[5] and all of them—close to two *billion* people!—are at risk for developing the disease.

In the late 1980s health experts began to notice a disturbing trend. For the first time in years, the number of cases of tuberculosis in the United States was increasing—and sometimes the drugs that used to cure TB did not work. Now doctors are worried that tuberculosis may once again become a major problem in America. Meanwhile, the same thing is happening in other leading nations, too.

A 1992 editorial in a scientific journal pointed out that "the 1990s is shaping up to be the decade of TB, much as the 1980s was the decade of AIDS."[6] While doctors battle what may be the return of the white plague, health officials are also battling another epidemic—fear of TB. In 1990 the writer of an article in *New York* magazine described a friend who was afraid of riding the city's subways in case a homeless person might cough on her and give her TB.[7] By 1992 New York City police officers were demanding protective masks, New York's correction workers union was suing the city demanding TB protection, and health care workers were threatening to shut down the city's hospitals.[8] This fear is spreading, particularly in large cities where most TB cases occur.

Just how bad is the TB epidemic in America? Are *you* at risk? What can you do to make sure you don't get TB? These are important questions, and this book will help to answer them and many other concerns about one of the world's oldest and most feared diseases.

2

TB Through the Ages

J ohn Keats is remembered as one of the world's greatest poets. This nineteenth-century romantic told the woman he loved that they couldn't get married until he proved he could make a living as a poet. Keats's third book of poems earned him international fame, but it was too late. While caring for his brother who was ill with tuberculosis, Keats himself came down with the disease. He went to Rome, hoping that the warm climate would help him to recover, but he died there. He was only twenty-six. "A thing of beauty is a joy forever," Keats wrote. The world will never know how much more beauty he could have created if it weren't for TB.

The Start of TB

Tuberculosis has been around as long as there have been people—scientists have found signs of tuberculosis in the skeletal

11

remains of prehistoric humans.[1] The Babylonians described symptoms of tuberculosis on stone tablets more than two thousand years ago.[2] The mummy of the Egyptian pharaoh Tutankhamen, who died in 1352 B. C., shows that he had tuberculosis, and the ancient Egyptians are believed to have had a large sanatorium where tuberculosis sufferers were treated.[3]

The ancient Greeks called tuberculosis *phthisis*, from their word for "to waste away." The swollen glands that may appear in the necks of TB sufferers gave another name to the disease: *scrofula*, which literally means "like a nursing sow (a female pig)." In Europe, until the eighteenth century, tuberculosis was also known as the King's Evil and it was believed that the touch of a king could cure the disease. The term *tuberculosis*

FAMOUS PEOPLE
WHO SUFFERED FROM TB

Writers: Charlotte and Emily Brontë, Lord Byron, Anton Chekhov, Ralph Waldo Emerson, John Keats, D. H. Lawrence, Molière, Eugene O'Neill, Edgar Allan Poe, Percy Bysshe Shelley, Robert Louis Stevenson

Musicians: Frédéric Chopin, Wolfgang Amadeus Mozart

Artists: Aubrey Beardsley, Paul Gauguin, Amedeo Modigliani

Philosophers/Theologians: Baruch Spinoza, Voltaire, John Calvin

Others: Simon Bolívar, W. C. Fields, Ulysses S. Grant, Vivien Leigh, Eleanor Roosevelt, Tutankhamen

first appeared in print around 1840, but it was not widely used until the turn of the century.[4]

Throughout human history, tuberculosis has been a leading cause of death. Ancient Greek records claimed this disease as the worst of all diseases at that time. In the mid-1600s in London, one out of five deaths was due to this dreaded disease. In the 1700s and 1800s one out of four Europeans died of "consumption."[5] Even in America, tuberculosis was one of the major killers until this century.

Tracking Down the Cause of TB

Nearly 2,300 years ago, the famous Greek philosopher Aristotle said that tuberculosis could be spread from one person to another. He was right, but through the ages this view went in and out of favor. At various times it was believed that the disease was caused by an unhealthy climate, impure air, unsanitary food, a tumor, mental depression, or damp soil; or that it was brought on by other diseases such as typhoid fever and measles.

Because some famous artists and writers died from tuberculosis, it was popularly believed in the 1800s that there was a link between TB and creativity. Some people thought that TB was an inherited trait that appeared in geniuses. Others believed that the disease actually helped artists, writers, and musicians to think more clearly. In fact, it was almost fashionable to have consumption. When Keats came down with the disease, his friend and fellow writer Shelley comforted him by saying, "This consumption is a disease particularly fond of people who write such good verses as you have done."[6]

Consumption was glamorized in the arts and literature of the time. Tragic heroes and heroines died a brave, lingering death from this disease. Today many people think that a tanned complexion is the picture of health, but the standard of attractiveness in the nineteenth century was the pale and delicate appearance of the consumptive. Though the disease was glamorized, it was still greatly feared. When the composer Chopin moved to the island of Majorca in the Mediterranean, people there panicked because he had the disease. Doctors often avoided listing tuberculosis on death records, to spare the victim's family unpleasant repercussions. (Today's doctors may avoid listing AIDS in death records for very similar reasons.) Because TB was popularly thought to be hereditary, relatives could have difficulty making a good marriage, be barred from certain occupations, and be unable to obtain life insurance.

Tuberculosis was believed to be inherited because it so often affected many members of the same family. The nineteenth-century writer Ralph Waldo Emerson, for example, lost his first wife to TB, and he himself, his brothers, other family members, and descendants had the disease as well. Tuberculosis also ran in the Keats, Brontë, and Thoreau families.[7]

In 1865 Jean Antoine Villemin, a French military surgeon, put the idea that TB was inherited to rest once and for all. He took pus and fluid from human TB patients and infected cows with TB and transferred the fluids to rabbits.

The rabbits promptly developed tuberculosis. If the disease could be passed from a human to a rabbit, obviously it was not hereditary.

In 1882 Robert Koch discovered the *tubercle bacillus*, a rod-shaped bacterium that is the cause of the disease. Koch was a German physician who helped establish bacteriology as a separate science. He developed methods of staining and culturing (growing) bacteria that are still used today in the study of bacteria that cause infection. One of his greatest achievements was the discovery of the tubercle bacillus. After trying 271 times to culture the organism that caused TB, Dr. Koch finally saw the rod-shaped bacteria. He found the organisms in samples taken from eleven patients with severe TB, as well as from cattle, chickens, guinea pigs, monkeys, and rabbits.[8] In honor of his discovery, the bacterium is sometimes called Koch's bacillus.

Koch also prepared an extract from dead tubercle bacilli called *tuberculin,* which he had hoped would work as a vaccination against the disease. He was disappointed with the results, but the extract proved valuable as a test for helping to determine whether or not a person had been exposed to the tuberculosis-causing bacteria. Koch was awarded a Nobel Prize in medicine in 1905 for his work with tuberculosis.

Searching For a Cure

Koch was not the first person to search for a cure for TB. During the first 200 years A.D., Roman TB sufferers were urged by their physicians to take long sea voyages. The open air and salty breezes were supposed to improve the condition. Some travelled south to Mount Vesuvius, near Naples, to breathe in volcanic fumes; others inhaled the smoke of burning cow dung, ate mice boiled in oil, or drank elephant's blood. Because doctors could offer no real hope, many people turned to these and other "miracle cures." But none of them worked. The only thing doctors could recommend was plenty of rest and fresh air.

In the early part of this century most people with tuberculosis went to a live-in facility called a sanatorium to recover. The first sanatorium for TB patients was opened in 1859 in a pine forest in the mountains of Silesia in eastern Europe by Hermann Brehmer, a German botanist. Brehmer had recovered from tuberculosis while on a plant-collecting trip to the Himalayas, and he believed that fresh air, plenty of rest, exercise, and good food would "dry out" the lungs and cure the disease.

A quarter century later, in 1885, the first TB sanatorium in the United States was opened by Edward L. Trudeau in the Adirondack Mountains of New York. By the early 1900s there were more than 400 TB sanatoriums in the United States.[9]

Sanatoriums helped keep people with tuberculosis out of crowded areas, which helped to slow down the spread of the disease. But were they effective? Although many patients recovered, thanks to this treatment of fresh air and plenty of rest, between 1900 and 1950 five million Americans died from tuberculosis.[10]

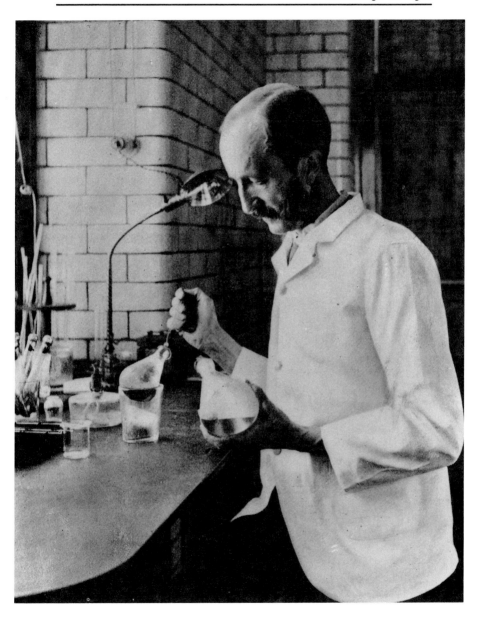

Dr. Edward L. Trudeau at work in his laboratory. Dr. Trudeau opened the first TB sanatorium in the United States in 1885.

These TB patients at a sanatorium slept outdoors. Fresh air and sunshine were thought to be the best treatment for tuberculosis.

The Rise of Anti-Tuberculosis Societies

Once Koch proved that tuberculosis was spread by germs, reformers had new ammunition. The industrial revolution had created a harsh environment for the working classes of the world. They lived in insanitary, crowded quarters, with contaminated water and limited food supply. Since TB, the most dreaded of diseases, was spread under just such conditions, it therefore benefited everyone to improve the standard of living of the common person.

In the late 1800s groups began springing up around the world to fight tuberculosis. In Austria in 1890 a Society for the Establishment of Sanatoria for the Consumptive Poor was founded. The following year in Denmark the National League for the Campaign against Tuberculosis was formed. Similar societies were set up all across Europe. In 1904 the National Association for the Study and Prevention of Tuberculosis was organized in the United States. Many other anti-tuberculosis organizations were also formed throughout the country.

In 1907 TB was America's number-one killer disease, claiming 156,000 victims each year. By 1940 the American population had increased 50 percent, but only 60,000 people died of TB that year, and tuberculosis had fallen to seventh place among the killer diseases.

The Age of Antibiotics

In the 1940s antibiotics were developed that were effective against tuberculosis bacteria. Streptomycin, for example, first

CHRISTMAS SEALS

One of the ways people collected money to stamp out TB was by using Christmas Seals. The idea started in Denmark, where a postal clerk named Einar Holboell thought of selling special Christmas stamps to raise money to fight TB. In 1907 American Red Cross volunteer Emily Bissell read an article about the special stamps and used this idea to raise $3,000 for her local Delaware tuberculosis society. The following year the Red Cross expanded Christmas Seals to a national effort, and it was a huge success, raising $135,000. In 1909 the Red Cross joined forces with the National Association for the Study and Prevention of Tuberculosis (NASPT) to sell Christmas Seals, and raised $250,000. NASPT eventually became the National Tuberculosis Association, and in 1919 it took over the management of Christmas Seals sales. By 1929 sales had reached $5.5 million.

As TB became less of a problem, the National Tuberculosis Association shifted its focus to include other respiratory diseases, and its name was changed to the National Tuberculosis and Respiratory Disease Association. In 1973 it was changed again to the American Lung Association. By the early 1990s Christmas Seals sales were close to $40 million each year—the largest nonprofit direct mail campaign in America.[11]

became available in 1947. After that, the death rate from TB dropped dramatically—from 33 per 100,000 population in 1947 down to 0.5 per 100,000 by the mid-1980s.[12]

Society had made a lot of progress in preventing the disease from spreading. Now, for the first time, doctors had real hope of saving most of the people who got the disease, which slowed down its spread even more.

The United States started a vigorous campaign to wipe out the disease. Children were tested for TB in schools. Doctors and nurses were highly trained to diagnose tuberculosis. People could receive free chest X-rays from travelling vans. During 1953 there were 84,000 new cases of tuberculosis, and in 1954 110,000 beds were being used for tuberculosis cases.[13] Between 1953 and 1984 the number of TB cases reported decreased about 5 percent a year—down to 22,000 new cases a year in 1984; by the mid-1980s less than 1,600 people were dying from TB each year in America.

TB Is Increasing

Then in 1985 the downward trend stopped. In 1986 the number of new cases went up. They've been going up ever since. In 1991 there were 26,283 new cases, almost 20 percent more than in 1984. Since 1984 thirty-one states have reported increases in numbers of cases of tuberculosis.[14] Early in 1992 the American Lung Association predicted that if the problem continues at the current rate, the number of new cases of TB will practically double by the year 2000—to 50,000 a year.[15]

Concerned about the increase in tuberculosis, in 1989, Secretary of Health and Human Services Louis W. Sullivan set 2010 as the target date for eliminating TB in the United States. But now many health officials are worried about regaining control over tuberculosis, let alone being able to wipe it out. And people are panicking as news stories about outbreaks of TB are becoming ever more common.

TB Today

3

Dealers working on the exchange floor of the World Trade Center in New York had some unscheduled excitement one summer day in 1992. Active TB had been diagnosed in two employees, and now everyone was required to take a tuberculin test. Only staff members wearing a sticker showing they had tested negative would be allowed back on the exchange floor.[1] Actually, health experts believe that these new rules were an overreaction, and most World Trade Center workers had little risk of getting the disease. But the incident vividly pointed up the fact that TB is a growing problem today, affecting more lives each year.

"At no time in recent history has tuberculosis been of such great concern as it is now, and legitimately so, because tuberculosis is out of control in this country," says Dr. Dixie Snider, of the Centers for Disease Control in Atlanta.[2]

What happened? How did a problem that seemed to be disappearing turn into a crisis so suddenly? And why did it happen now?

A New Resurgence

America had become overconfident about tuberculosis. After the development of effective antibiotics, the number of TB cases dropped dramatically—so much, in fact, that doctors and government officials no longer considered it an important health problem. As Dr. Dixie Snider admits, "We made a mistake—we thought we had all the tools we needed to conquer TB."[3] But by the mid-1980s many of these needed tools were gone. All the TB sanatoriums had been closed down; it was easier just to treat patients on an outpatient basis. Cities and states had cut back on their programs; TB clinics were closed and funding for TB screening was cut. Some medical schools barely taught about the disease, except as a lesson in medical history. The health care structure that had been built up to wipe out this most dreaded of diseases had been largely dismantled.

Even when health experts became aware of the growing threat, there seemed to be no sense of urgency. In 1989 the Department of Health and Human Services (HHS) came up with a plan to eliminate TB. The Centers for Disease Control estimated that it would cost about $30 to $40 million a year. But the HHS did not ask for the money that year, and in 1990 and 1991 it requested only the $7 to $12 million it had already been spending for TB programs. "For a disease that was targeted to be eliminated by the year 2010, we're going backwards," was the comment of Dr. Beth Raucher, an epidemiologist at New York's Beth Israel Medical Center.[4] Finally, in 1992, the HHS requested $28 million for TB programs. But it is much easier to contain a problem before it gets out of hand. Now the American Lung Association estimates it will cost *$90 million* to bring TB under control.

"We knew how to cure it. We had it in our hands. But we dropped the ball,"[5] says Dr. Michael Iseman of the National Jewish Center for Immunology and Respiratory Medicine in Denver. Without an aggressive program to prevent TB, doctors were simply relying on antibiotics to cure any cases that arose. But back in the early 1950s René and Jean Dubos had written a book called *The White Plague* in which they warned health officials that it was dangerous to believe that antibiotics alone could keep TB under control. They pointed out that the greatest advances against the disease arose from improved sanitation and living conditions from the late 1800s onward, which helped to keep TB from spreading as much in the first place.[6] Indeed, after antibiotics were available, tuberculosis was found mainly among the poor, because antibiotics were not accessible to them.

In the 1980s several important factors contributed to the new rise in TB. This was a decade of increased drug abuse, HIV and AIDS, homelessness, poverty, and an influx of new immigrants—just the right conditions to spread tuberculosis. And yet, "Even if bad things like HIV and homelessness hadn't occurred, TB would have come back. People have treated this as a great surprise, but it's a predictable result of abandoning public health measures that were working," says Dr. Barry R. Bloom, professor of microbiology and immunology at Albert Einstein College of Medicine in New York and the top TB adviser to the World Health Organization.[7]

The spread of AIDS had a tremendous impact on the growing TB problem. People infected with the HIV virus that causes AIDS are more susceptible to other diseases, too—especially TB—because their ravaged immune systems can't provide the proper defenses to fight off diseases. Homeless people and intravenous drug users are two high-risk populations for HIV. In the crowded quarters that exist in shelters or in prisons, TB bacteria are able to spread even faster. "We have re-created the conditions in which TB was spread in the nineteenth century," points out Dr. Karen Brudney of Harlem Hospital Center in New York[8]. The AIDS virus is causing a huge surge in TB worldwide. The World Health Organization estimates that three million HIV-infected people may also be infected with TB. In sub-Saharan Africa 30 to 40 percent of all hospital admissions are TB-related.

Another important factor: it isn't just the "normal" type of tuberculosis that is spreading. Strains of tuberculosis that are resistant to drug treatment have become more common, so that doctors are having more difficulty curing many of the new cases. By early 1992 seventeen states had recorded cases of drug-resistant TB. In one study as many as one-third of recent TB cases in New York City were resistant to drugs. In recent outbreaks, between 50 and 80 percent of those with multidrug-resistant strains of TB have died! (Normally, as many as 98 percent of TB cases can be cured when treated promptly.) Most of these people had started out with "regular" TB but did not complete their drug treatments. As a result, TB bacilli that were not killed by the medications they had started taking multiplied in their bodies, producing drug-resistant infections.

Currently 90 percent of the patients with multidrug-resistant strains have the HIV virus, but if drug-resistant TB keeps spreading, other populations may be affected. "My greatest concern is that multiple-drug-resistant TB will continue to escalate and then we will be in a situation where we will have, in fact, lost the ability to actually treat and cure," says Dr. Margaret A. Hamburg, acting city health commissioner of New York.[9] Experts such as Dr. Anthony S. Fauci, the director of the National Institute of Allergy and Infectious Diseases and one of the top federal AIDS scientists, suggest that the spread of drug-resistant tuberculosis could become as serious a threat to public health as AIDS. Says Dr. Fauci, "This is really a déja vù of 1981 when we were talking about a strange new immunodeficiency disease [AIDS], and people were saying we were being alarmist. The problem is [that] when we say these things we get accused of being hysterical and crying wolf."[10]

An increase in the number of immigrants to the United States from places where tuberculosis is common is also contributing to the rise in TB cases. In 1991 27 percent of all new TB cases in the United States occurred in those who were born in another country.

TB Is Spread in Crowded Places

Tuberculosis has the best chance to spread in places where many people are crowded together, such as homeless shelters and prisons, hospitals, schools, and nursing homes.

- Twelve homeless men who were staying at a homeless shelter in New York City in 1990 contracted the same strain of tuberculosis.

- More than a dozen inmates and a guard died in outbreaks of drug-resistant TB at several New York State prisons in 1991.

- According to a *New York Newsday* report, by early 1992 at least 100 patients had caught drug-resistant TB in New York City hospitals, and 65 had died from it.[11]

- In Prince Georges County, Maryland, in 1990, twenty-one students at two public schools were found to be infected with TB.

- Studies have found that nursing-home residents are from five to thirty times more likely to develop TB than similar-aged people living at home.

TB Has Retreated Into Pockets

Tuberculosis is not yet a problem that affects everyone. "TB has retreated into pockets—the foreign-born, intravenous-drug users, the medically underserved, residents of long-term facilities such as prisons and nursing homes, and people with HIV infection," says Dr. George Di Ferdinando, medical director for New York State's TB control programs.[12]

But the people who spend a lot of time with those with tuberculosis are also at risk for contracting the disease. Not only family members but also doctors and nurses, police and prison guards, and workers in homeless shelters, drug treatment centers, and nursing homes may have daily contact with TB sufferers. A 1992 study found that an alarming number of health care workers in large inner-city hospitals were infected with tuberculosis. Twelve out of twenty-six doctors who had previously had a negative skin test now had a positive reaction. This is an infection rate of 46 percent.[13] At Woodhull Hospital in Brooklyn, a survey released in 1992 showed that seventy-eight staff members who had tested negative for TB in 1990 tested positive for the disease in 1991.[14] A *New York Newsday* report found that by early 1992, nineteen health care workers had contracted drug-resistant TB while on the job in New York City, and six had died.[15]

AIDS was once isolated mainly in homosexuals, IV drug users, and people who had had blood transfusions. Now it is a problem that affects everyone. Unless the spread of TB is brought under control, it could become a major threat to the general public, too.

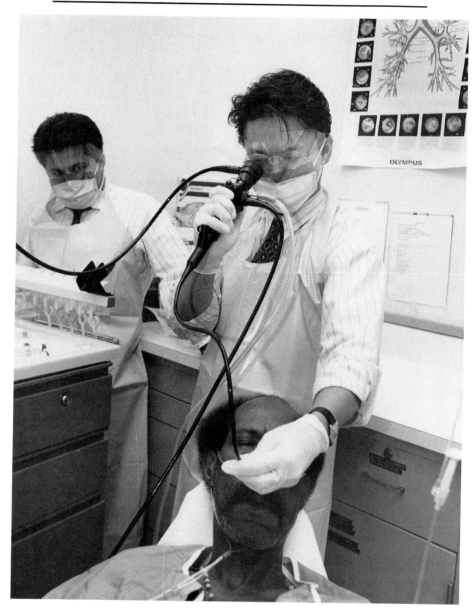

Doctors, nurses, and other health care workers are at increased risk for contracting TB. At one New York hospital, the infection rate was 46 percent.

The U.S. TB Epidemic

Overall, about ten people out of every 100,000 in America have tuberculosis. But most of the outbreaks of TB occur in large inner-city areas such as Atlanta, San Francisco, New York, and Newark, New Jersey. Many of these cities now have from five to seven times the national average of TB cases.

"Fifteen cases per 100,000 population, or fifty cases in a county is an epidemic," says Dr. Charles Felton, chief of the pulmonary division at New York's Harlem Hospital Center. "The case rate for New York City as a whole is about fifty per 100,000, but some middle-class neighborhoods have rates below the national average. Central Harlem has the highest rate in the

WHO IS AT GREATEST RISK TODAY?

People who are:
- HIV-infected
- homeless
- IV drug users
- prisoners
- nursing-home residents

Those who work in:
- hospitals
- prisons
- homeless shelters
- nursing homes
- drug treatment centers

TB is more common:
- among men than women
- among African Americans and Latinos than other ethnic groups
- in people aged 25 to 44 than any other age group

United States: 233 cases per 100,000 population. That's a Third World level."[16] Because of undercounting and underreporting, experts believe the actual number of Americans with TB is 20 to 40 percent higher.

TB rates are actually higher in some parts of American society than in the poorest countries in the world. In sub-Saharan Africa where TB is a major killer, and among young black men in New York City, the case rate is the same: about 350 cases per 100,000. Tuberculosis is not confined to America's big cities, however; other areas where TB has not previously been a problem are now being affected. In 1989, for example, Wyoming reported no cases of TB, but in 1990 there were five.

 FACTS FROM AROUND THE NATION[17]

- Atlanta had the most cases of TB in 1991: 76 cases per 100,000 residents. Georgia's Governor Zell Miller authorized spending $300,000 from his emergency fund to expand hospital facilities for TB patients.
- At the A. G. Holly Hospital in Lantana, north of Miami, all 120 beds were full in the summer of 1991 and each one held a TB patient.
- In San Francisco, the city with the sixth highest rate of TB in 1990, AIDS and intravenous drugs were blamed for the increase. A methadone program for heroin addicts currently includes medication to prevent TB.

Young People Are at Risk

One of the most alarming findings for health officials is that the number of children with tuberculosis is increasing. In 1989 the number of childhood cases of TB in the nation rose 16 percent. In New York City the number nearly doubled between 1989 and 1990. More than two-thirds were four years old or younger. "We see a significant increase in TB in preschool children whose parents are sexually active and using drugs," says Dr. Felton of the Harlem Hospital Center.[18] A study conducted by Dr. Laura Inselman of the Newington Children's Hospital in Connecticut found that minority children are being increasingly exposed to adults with HIV who also have TB. In fact, 80 percent of childhood cases occur in minority groups.

TB Risk Has Changed Over the Years

Tuberculosis is often linked with poverty, but it can strike anyone at any age. Before the age of antibiotics, young women had the highest TB mortality rate. After antibiotics were available, the chance of infection in childhood decreased, and the elderly had the greatest risk of developing active tuberculosis. Young adults are now the group with the most rapidly rising TB rate. "These are people with HIV, drug abusers, people living in shelters or on the streets," says Barry Bloom, professor of microbiology and immunology at New York's Albert Einstein College of Medicine.[19]

"[Our] CDC data show that, by race and ethnicity, the

largest increases in TB cases from 1985 to 1990 occurred among Hispanics, 55 percent; blacks, 27 percent; and Asians, 20 percent. The increases . . . are probably due in large part to the HIV epidemic, which similarly affects these minority populations," says Dr. William Roper, director of the Centers for Disease Control Public Health Service.[20]

4

What Is Tuberculosis?

The doctors at Massachusetts General Hospital were puzzled. Their seventeen-year-old patient was a girl from Cambodia, who had come to the United States six years before. She looked healthy, although a little thin, and she didn't have a fever or any other obvious symptoms. But she was complaining of a severe pain in her abdomen. It had been coming and going, every day or two, for the past few months; now it hurt so much that she couldn't sleep. When the doctors examined her, they could feel a small, firm mass in her lower right abdomen. Could it be appendicitis? Or perhaps a bowel inflammation or intestinal parasites? Maybe it was a tumor. Intestinal tuberculosis was another possibility, because the girl had a positive tuberculin skin test when she first arrived in this country. The doctors didn't think TB was very

35

likely—the patient's chest x-ray was normal, and tests of her sputum showed no signs of TB bacteria. But when the pain continued to get worse, the doctors operated and found clear signs of intestinal tuberculosis. TB bacteria were also found in nearby lymph nodes.[1]

This was not a "typical" case of tuberculosis, as it occurs in the United States today. The more common lung infections often used to be linked with intestinal TB, but now the abdominal form is found mainly in Asian immigrants. It is usually due to drinking unpasteurized milk, which may contain *Mycobacterium bovis*, a germ that causes TB in cows.

At the turn of the century, almost all children living in large cities in Europe were infected with tuberculosis-causing bacteria. Today, over 1.7 billion people worldwide, including ten to fifteen million Americans, have been infected. Fortunately, infection does not always lead to coming down with the disease. If it did, humans would have been wiped out by tuberculosis a long time ago.

Causes of TB

Tuberculosis is caused by several different species of microscopic rod-shaped organisms that belong to a group of bacteria called *mycobacteria*. Mycobacteria have characteristics similar to bacteria and fungi. The species that cause tuberculosis in humans are *Mycobacterium tuberculosis* (the human type) and *Mycobacterium bovis* (which affects cows). Tuberculosis-causing bacteria are called *tubercle bacilli*.

Mycobacteria are very small—from about 0.5 to 4

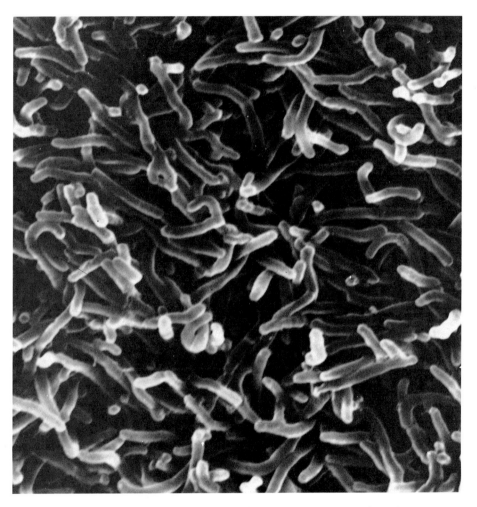

Mycobacterium bovis cells (which affects cows) as scanned under an electron microscope. These cells are magnified approximately 6000 times their actual size.

microns, which is about 1/50,000 to 1/6,000 of an inch. Tubercle bacilli do not grow in soil or water like some other bacteria. They must be passed from one human or animal carrier to another. They are aerobic, which means they must have oxygen to live. Other domestic animals such as pigs and chickens also get tuberculosis. The type that causes lung disease in chickens (*Mycobacterium avium*) does not usually affect humans, but for people with AIDS it may be a serious problem. TB is not very common in wild animals and birds.

There are more than fifty different types of mycobacteria. It is estimated that forty million Americans have been infected with non-tuberculosis mycobacteria. Some cause illnesses in humans, but many do not. Besides TB, the best known mycobacterium is *Mycobacterium leprae*, which causes leprosy.

How People Get TB

When someone with active tuberculosis coughs or sneezes, or even talks, sings, or laughs, tuberculosis bacteria are carried into the air in tiny droplets of moisture. A sneeze may release as many as forty million microscopic droplets. There can be hundreds of bacilli in a single drop. Heavy droplets fall to the ground, but the smallest (as tiny as 1/5,000 of an inch) evaporate, and the tiny tubercle bacilli drift through the air like dust. (Tubercle bacilli can survive out of the body for a long time—as much as thirty years—and they can withstand extreme cold and heat.) The disease is spread when someone breathes in the bacilli.

This is the main way that people get TB today, but they

can also become infected by eating food that is contaminated with the bacteria, or by drinking milk from cows with the disease. *M. bovis* most often causes TB in bones and joints. At one time, one out of every twenty milk cows in America was infected with *M. bovis.* Today this mycobacterium rarely causes TB in America and other developed countries because the bacteria are killed when milk is pasteurized, and animals are routinely tested for various diseases including TB. It is still a problem in some parts of the world, however—and among immigrants from those areas, such as the Cambodian-American girl whose story was told at the beginning of the chapter.

Coming in contact with a TB germ does not necessarily mean you will become infected. There are germs all around us all the time, but the body can successfully fight off most of them. Our skin keeps most germs out of the body, although some can get through when the skin is cut. There are bacteria and other germs in the food we eat, but strong stomach acids kill most of them. Our noses filter out many of the germs that are in the air we breathe. When a germ gets past these body defenses and penetrates into body tissues, it produces an infection. But even having an infection doesn't necessarily mean we will become ill. The body has further defenses inside the body, too.

Out of one hundred people who are exposed to TB bacteria, only twenty-five will become infected, and most of those infected will never get the disease. Only three out of the twenty-five will develop active cases of tuberculosis.

When the body's immune defenses are not working properly, the risk of going from TB infection to active disease increases sharply. That is why so many TB cases are occurring among people with AIDS.

What Happens Inside the Body

What happens if a person breathes in tubercle bacilli? The respiratory system is protected by a layer of mucus that lines the nasal passages and the tracheobronchial tree, whose "trunk" is the trachea or windpipe, a thick, muscular tube that divides into two main branches (bronchi); each of these, in turn, branches into smaller tubes, leading to hundreds of thousands

RISK VARIES WITH AGE

Infants are very susceptible to developing active tuberculosis when they are exposed to family members who have the disease. Young children up to age five have twice as much risk of developing active disease as adults have. Adolescents and young adults also have a high risk of developing active tuberculosis. Children older than five who have not yet reached puberty and middle-aged adults seem to be more resistant. In old age, though, susceptibility rises again.

of tiny airways called bronchioles that spread throughout the lungs. The bronchioles end in tiny air sacs called alveoli in the lungs. It is here that oxygen is delivered to tiny blood vessels in the alveolar walls.

Foreign particles, including bacteria, are trapped in the sticky mucus in the airways. Underneath the layer of mucus are cells with tiny hairlike projections called cilia. The cilia wave back and forth together, producing currents that push mucus and the particles trapped in it toward the throat. There the mucus can be coughed up, harmlessly swallowed, sneezed, or blown out into a tissue. (The combination of saliva, mucus, and cell waste products that is coughed up from the lungs is called *sputum*.)

If some of the tubercle bacilli get past this protection system and make it to the alveolar sacs deep in the lungs, a primary infection may result. Primary infection is the first stage in the development of tuberculosis, but it does not always lead to the disease.

The amount of time between infection and actual illness can vary greatly among TB patients and is often, in fact, quite long. In the past it was thought that there were two different diseases: "primary" TB (sometimes called childhood tuberculosis because it generally occurred in children) and "post-primary" tuberculosis, which occurs long after a primary infection. The second type has also been called "adult" or "reinfective" or "reactivation" or "active" tuberculosis because it is a reactivation of a primary infection.

The First Stage of Tuberculosis

Scientists believe that tubercle bacilli that enter the alveolar sacs are quickly attacked by the body's defense system. Large amoebalike cells called alveolar macrophages engulf the bacteria. Most other bacteria are easily broken down inside the macrophages. But the tuberculosis bacteria are protected by a thick waxy coating. "What you have is a virtual grease ball that is impervious," says Dr. Patrick Brennan, a researcher at Colorado State University in Fort Collins.[2] Many of the bacteria are killed, but some of the tubercle bacilli are able to survive and even continue multiplying inside the macrophages.

Bacilli-containing macrophages start to clump together inside the alveolar sac where infection has occurred. T cells and other white blood cells join the clump to battle with the invaders. Within several weeks after the initial infection, the clumped cells have formed a small, hard, gray swelling called a *tubercle.* The T cells produce chemical messengers that activate the macrophages to kill TB bacilli or stop them from growing. But these protective reactions also damage some of the lung cells.

The tubercle may gradually grow larger, destroying lung tissue around it. Soft, cheeselike areas are formed inside the tubercle as cells die. On the outside, tough scar tissue forms to surround the tubercle. The bacilli are trapped inside this wall of scar tissue, like prisoners in a jail cell. They remain alive, but they stop multiplying. In most cases a person with a primary infection does not feel any symptoms, and the

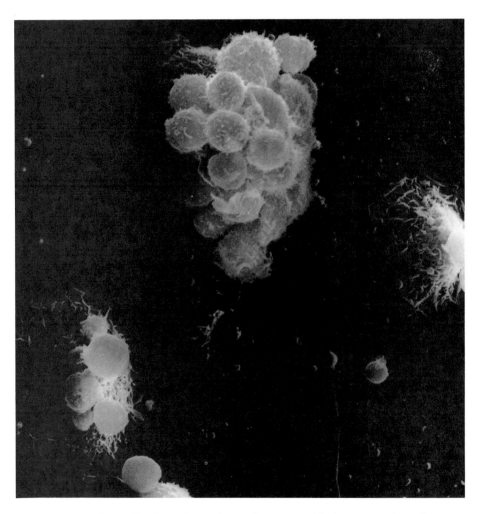

Macrophages (such as those shown here, magnified at approximately 1040 times actual size) work to break down bacteria in the body. While most bacteria are easily broken down, the TB are protected by a thick waxy coating.

infection goes undetected. But sometimes fever, rash, or nausea may occur. At this stage, when the disease is still contained in the primary infection, the person is not contagious and cannot transmit TB to others.

The Entire Body May Be Affected

A primary infection is not yet the disease of tuberculosis. Ironically, TB may be spread by the body's own disease-fighting cells. Some of the bacilli-filled macrophages are carried out of the body in the mucus, but others may be transported into another part of the lungs. The lymph system may carry them to nearby lymph nodes; or the blood system may spread them throughout the body.

In cases in the United States today, TB affects the lungs about 90 percent of the time, producing the form called *pulmonary tuberculosis.* But nearly every part of the body can be affected: the bones and joints, the brain, the skin, throat, intestines, liver, genital organs, kidneys, bladder, and lymph nodes. Two of the most serious complications are miliary tuberculosis and tuberculosis meningitis.

Miliary tuberculosis. In fewer than one percent of TB cases the primary infection is not contained and the organisms spread into the blood system, causing miliary tuberculosis. Early investigators thought that the small nodules formed as tubercle bacilli became implanted throughout the body looked like millet seeds. The Latin word for millet is *milium,* hence the term *miliary.* Miliary tuberculosis causes a high fever, and without drugs it is usually fatal. Even with drugs, from 5 to 35 percent of patients may die. Before antibiotics, miliary tuberculosis was most common in children, but now it most often occurs among the elderly.

TB meningitis. Tuberculosis meningitis also occurred primarily in children in the past, but it, too, has shifted to become a disease of the elderly. Unlike most forms of TB, tubercular meningitis progresses very rapidly. Half of all patients have been sick for only two weeks before they are diagnosed. Meningitis causes an inflammation in the coverings of the brain and spinal chord. Symptoms include headache, fever, and seizures; coma and death may occur if the disease is not treated. Before drug treatment was available for TB, nearly all cases were fatal. Now four out of five patients are saved.

Post-Primary Tuberculosis

Only one out of ten TB cases develops directly from a primary infection into an active case of tuberculosis. In 90 percent of the cases, tuberculosis develops after the primary infection has been contained. (Remember that people with a primary TB infection, contained in tubercles in the lungs, usually have no symptoms and may not realize they are infected.) The disease occurs if the tubercle bacilli become active again. Infants, children, the elderly, or people with other illnesses may develop tuberculosis soon after a primary infection but in most cases it does not develop until a long time afterward. About half of all TB cases develop within a year of primary infection, and the other half develop some time later in life. The bacilli are reactivated when the body's defenses are weakened, such as after another illness, or in old age.

When the TB bacteria become reactivated they break out of the tubercles and multiply. Tubercle bacilli grow rather slowly for bacteria. They reproduce every twelve to twenty hours, compared with common intestinal bacteria that can double their numbers in twenty minutes. Nevertheless, in ten days a single TB bacterium will have multiplied to 5,000—enough to create a nodule in the lung. In less than a month a single tubercle bacillus can produce one billion organisms, enough to cause a cavity in the lungs. Mycobacteria invade the surrounding lung tissue and

RISK OF REACTIVATION IS GREATEST:

- in the first two years after primary infection
- in infants, adolescents, and the elderly
- in those who have had inadequate treatment for TB
- in those who are immunologically impaired (for example, people who are HIV-infected, diabetic, or taking steroid drugs)

continue reproducing. They may break through the alveolar wall and enter a blood vessel or a lymph vessel. They may then be carried around to other parts of the body.

Pulmonary Tuberculosis

Tuberculosis of the lungs is called pulmonary tuberculosis, or post-primary pulmonary tuberculosis, and it is by far the most common form of TB. There are often no symptoms at first, or they may occur so gradually that they are not noticed. By the time they are noticed the disease is usually well established.

Sputum production and coughing are often the earliest symptoms of pulmonary tuberculosis. Alveolar macrophages and white blood cells start clumping together, and lung tissue breaks down and is replaced by a soft, cheeselike material. This may eventually become more liquid and is carried up the respiratory tract in the mucus, leaving behind cavities and scar tissue in the lungs. The secretions irritate the bronchi, causing coughing. At first this may occur only in the morning because material has accumulated in the bronchi overnight. There is not much sputum to begin with, but as the disease worsens it becomes more abundant. The cough is usually not very severe and is often mistaken for a cold that won't go away.

The first real sign that something may be wrong is often blood in the sputum (*hemoptysis*). This occurs when blood vessels in the lungs become damaged. As the disease worsens, the patient may cough up large amounts of blood. Other symptoms of advanced tuberculosis include chest pain,

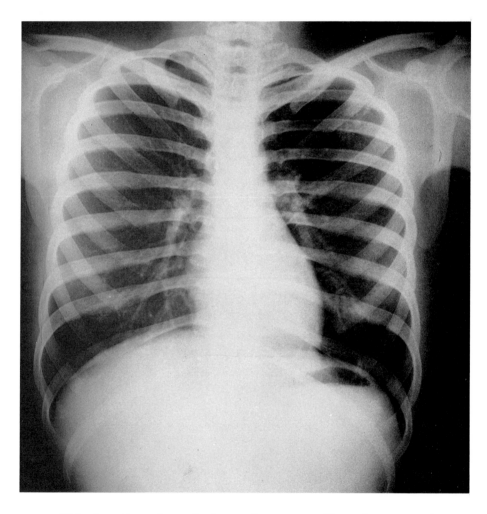

This chest X-ray shows the lungs of a patient suffering from minimal pulmonary tuberculosis.

fatigue, fever, loss of appetite, sweating at night, and weight loss. Eventually the disease may produce huge cavities and extensive scarring in the lungs. After a while there may not be enough healthy lung tissue left for effective breathing, and the person may die. Tuberculosis can cause death quickly, but more often it is a long-term disease that gradually gets worse.

TB Is Spread Indoors

TB germs are quickly killed outdoors by the sunlight's ultraviolet rays. Indoors, though, the tubercle bacilli dry out and float on air currents, and they can survive for a long time in a closed-in area. Fresh air from open windows and some air-conditioning systems will get rid of contaminating tubercle bacilli.

"However, since infectious tubercle bacilli remain suspended in the air, air-conditioning systems that recirculate air can concentrate and spread the infection," says Dr. Lee Reichman, director of the pulmonary division of the New Jersey Medical School in Newark and former president of the American Lung Association.[3] "TB spread is most likely when a person with active infection is crowded in with others for a long time—in a shelter, a prison, a school, a nursing home, a day-care center."[4]

Risk Factors for Getting TB

The risk of getting TB depends on how infectious the TB patient is, how concentrated the infectious organisms are in the air you share with him or her, and how long you are exposed.

Although TB is spread through the air like the common cold, it is much harder to get than a cold. The odds are very low that you can get the disease from a casual encounter—passing a TB sufferer on the street, sitting next to one on a train, or visiting a TB patient in the hospital.

"TB is not as easy to catch as measles or chicken pox. It takes close, prolonged contact in the home, in the workplace, in jails or hospitals, not in subways or elevators," says Dr. Margaret Hamburg, New York City's acting health commissioner.[5]

"Your risk depends on the length of time you share the air in close, intimate, prolonged contact with someone who has active TB," says Dr. H. William Harris, a TB expert at New York University Medical Center/Bellevue.[6] According to experts like Dr. Reichman, "It takes perhaps two months of 24-hours-a-day contact or six months of 8-hours-a-day contact with someone with untreated, active tuberculosis who is coughing tubercle bacilli into the air."[7]

However, the risk increases in certain settings. "Workers in shelters are converting [becoming TB-infected] after very little exposure. If you work in a shelter, the chances are better than even that you'll acquire the organism," says Dr. Jeffrey Laurence, director of the Laboratory for AIDS Virus Research at the Cornell University Medical College in New York City.[8]

According to the American Lung Association, TB is not usually transmitted through personal items such as clothing, bedding, or other things the TB patient may have touched.[9]

People who work in homeless shelters, such as those shown in this photo, are at an increased risk of contracting TB.

Dr. John Sbarbaro, a TB expert at the University of Colorado, says, "TB is spread strictly through the air. Gross as it sounds, you could eat a plate of TB germs and not get infected, because your stomach acids would kill them. You don't get TB from kissing or from sexual intercourse or toilet seats, either." Of course, spending a lot of time with someone with TB also exposes you to the air that person breathes which puts you at risk.[10]

Why Some People Get TB and Others Do Not

Although TB is not hereditary as early doctors thought, heredity does play a part in resistance to TB. In a series of tests with rabbits run between 1932 and 1960, M. B. Lurie showed that genetics played an important part in resistance to TB and the way the disease affects the body.

This inherited resistance is also seen in humans. The risk of contracting tuberculosis once infection occurs varies among different people in the world.

Among Caucasians from 5 to 10 percent of those infected will develop the disease at some time during their lives. But among Eskimos as many as 40 percent of those infected develop tuberculosis. Researchers believe that this difference is due to the history of the disease. Caucasians have been exposed to TB for many centuries, and over time they have built up a natural immunity to the disease. Only the more resistant survived and had children, while those who were more susceptible died off. Eskimos, however, have only encountered the tubercle bacillus within the past 100 years.

Native Americans and African Americans also have a higher rate of developing TB.

Sometimes, though, what seems to be heredity is more likely the action of environmental factors. Earlier in the century, for example, Irish immigrants had one of the highest TB rates in the United States. But once their living standards reached those of the general population, their TB rate dropped.

Intravenous drug users are at high risk for both TB and AIDS. The poor nutrition and living conditions typical of this group combine to lower their resistance to disease. But doctors believe that another factor is also operating. The talc that is used to "cut" drugs such as heroin and cocaine contains silica, which damages the lung tissues. This makes it easier for TB to develop. Those with the HIV virus have an extremely high risk of developing TB when infected. In fact, "If they don't die from something else first, virtually 100 percent of AIDS patients carrying TB bacteria will develop the illness," says Dr. Michael Iseman of the National Jewish Center.[11] From 70 to 90 percent of multidrug-resistant TB–AIDS patients die, usually within weeks.

Other Factors

Doctors are still not sure about all the factors involved in why some people get TB and others don't. Many points are still being debated. For example, how many tubercle bacilli are needed to cause infection? Some studies have indicated it may take as little as seven bacteria to cause the disease, and there are tens of thousands of bacilli in a single cough from a highly contagious person.[12] In theory, a single bacterium could cause infection.

When is a patient no longer contagious? Often after about two weeks of drug treatment, tests show that there are no longer TB bacilli in the person's sputum. But sometimes people suffer a relapse shortly after that and become contagious once again. As researchers actively study the tubercle bacilli, many of the remaining questions will be cleared up.

5

Diagnosis

When Joyce was in college, there was an outbreak of tuberculosis in the city near the campus. But she didn't get sick, and it never occurred to her that she might have been infected. Years went by. She became a veterinarian, got married, settled down in Mississippi, and started raising a family. But then she caught what she thought was a bad cold. The nagging cough hung on, and the "cold" settled in her chest. Finally, fever and chest pain sent her to the doctor. A skin test was positive for TB infection, and then a sample of her sputum, grown in a laboratory culture dish, produced colonies of tubercle bacteria. Tests showed that Joyce's husband and two children were infected, too, although they did not have the active disease. Doctors put the whole family on antibiotics, which had to be continued for months. Joyce felt terrible when her two-year-old son cried each time he got his shots. "I'd be afraid to hold him because I felt dangerous," she says. "I felt guilty because I'd done this to my family."[1]

Most people are not diagnosed with TB right away, even when they have the active disease and are feeling ill. Dr. Dixie Snider, director of the Centers for Disease Control (CDC)'s division of tuberculosis control, says that "the usual story is that the patient has symptoms for three or four months before the diagnosis is made."[2] Even when patients are so sick that they have to be hospitalized, doctors don't always suspect TB. Instead, bronchitis, asthma, pneumonia, or a viral infection may be the first diagnosis.

Skin Tests

Most TB cases are first detected with a skin test. Within two to ten weeks after a primary infection, the body will become sensitized to the tubercle bacilli. Whenever it is exposed to the organism again, the body will be ready to fight it off. Doctors can use this fact to test for TB.

A small amount of tuberculin (a liquid made from the tubercle bacillus) is injected under the skin. If a person has been exposed to the tubercle bacilli, a swelling will develop around the spot where the skin test is given.

However, a person who has only recently been exposed to TB bacteria may not have a positive reaction for several weeks. So the result of the test will be a false negative; likewise, the test may give a false positive if a person has been exposed to a bacterium that is related but that does not cause TB.

Skin tests are the most useful tool for screening large populations, but the test only indicates that a person has been exposed to the TB bacillus. It doesn't show whether the organism is active.

Two types of tuberculin are available for skin tests—OT (old tuberculin) and PPD (purified protein derivative). OT is a filtrate of sterile, killed tubercle bacilli, which originally was developed by Koch. It is administered with a multiple-puncture device. This type of tuberculin is not used today.

PPD is a filtrate of OT. It can be administered in two ways. In the tine test it is given with a multipronged device. The tine test is still used in screening large populations, but there is no way to be sure how much of the tuberculin has been injected by this method. That is why experts believe the Mantoux test is more reliable. In the *Mantoux test*, a measured amount of PPD is injected under the skin and the area is examined two to three days later for swelling.

Chest X-ray

If a person has a positive skin test, chest X-rays may show tubercles or other signs of damage caused by tuberculosis in the lungs. Doctors might also discover tubercles when a chest X-ray is taken for some other reason.

The X-ray was discovered in 1895 by Wilhelm Conrad Roentgen, a German physicist. After a way to take X-ray

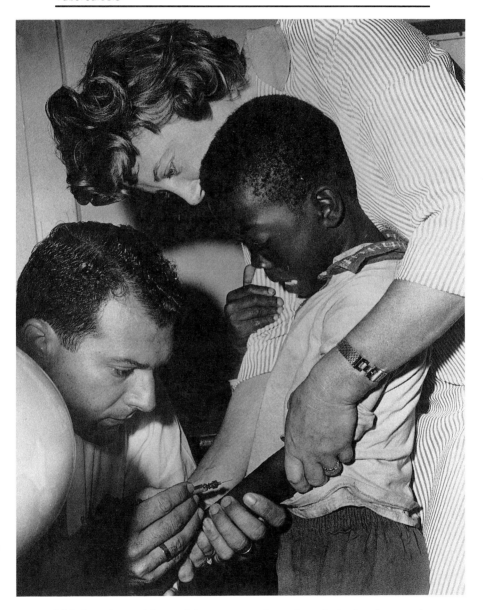

This boy is receiving a Mantoux test for tuberculosis. In the test, a measured amount of PPD is injected under the skin, and the area is examined two to three days later for swelling.

photographs cheaply was developed in 1936, X-rays were used to screen large numbers of people for tuberculosis. Today X-rays are no longer used for routine screening, because we now know that too many X-rays can increase the chances of cancer. So chest X-rays are usually taken only when a person has a positive TB skin test. A person whose immune system is damaged may not have a positive skin test even when an active TB infection is present, so in such cases a chest X-ray may be necessary.

Laboratory Tests

Even an X-ray may not be able to detect the presence of tuberculosis. Other lung infections might mask the disease, for example. If TB is suspected, it is confirmed by checking for the mycobacteria in the sputum (also called phlegm). Stomach contents can also be examined, since they contain sputum swallowed during the night. (This is true for children who cannot cough up sputum.) Samples of the fluid that cushions the brain and spinal cord may be examined if tubercular meningitis is suspected.

In the smear test, sputum samples are treated with chemicals and are then observed under the microscope. The chemicals used are called stains because they produce a colored spot if particular bacteria are present. But the stains used for the smear test can react not only with TB bacteria but also with some other kinds. So the test may give false positive results if the person has another bacterial infection.

Also, a negative result on the smear test does not

For many years after 1936, chest X-rays were used to screen large numbers of people for TB. Sometimes mobile X-ray units were set up, such as the one shown here, from the 1940s.

necessarily mean there are no TB bacteria present. There may not be enough of the bacteria for the test to detect. This means that the sputum sample must be "cultured." The sample is placed in laboratory dishes or test tubes under favorable conditions for bacteria to grow, to find out whether the bacteria are *Mycobacterium tuberculosis* or another kind of bacillus. Laboratory tests can also determine whether or not the bacilli are resistant to certain drugs, and which ones would be most effective for treatment. Unfortunately, tubercle bacilli grow so slowly that laboratory tests usually take from two to eight weeks to determine that they are present and from three to twelve weeks to establish which antibiotics will be most effective against them.

Sometimes it becomes necessary to do a bronchoscopy to obtain enough sputum or a lung biopsy to prove the diagnosis. A lighted tube (the bronchoscope) is inserted into the airways and samples of sputum are taken. Sometimes tiny bits of tissue must be taken from other organs (for example, lymph nodes, liver, or bone marrow) and cultured to show the presence of TB bacteria.

A new test that can yield a TB diagnosis in 24 hours or less was announced in 1992. It uses a technique called PCR (polymerase chain reaction) to identify the TB mycobacterium. Using PCR, a segment of the germ's DNA (the chemical carrying its hereditary information) is copied millions of times, which makes it possible to detect a single infected cell among thousands of uninfected cells. But this is a high-tech test, requiring special equipment and skilled technicians, and it would be too expensive to use for routine screening.

Who Should Be Tested?

It wasn't that long ago that all American children were routinely tested for TB in schools. Each child's forearm was punctured with a four-pronged device containing tuberculin and was examined a few days later for signs of a reaction (the tine test). As TB became less of a public threat, these testing programs were stopped. Because of recent outbreaks, some school systems have once again begun testing faculty and students for tuberculosis. The CDC now recommends that all school children be tested.[3]

TB skin testing is required in some states for immigrants and students, as well as for personnel who work in places

AIDS MAKES TB DIAGNOSIS HARDER

The recent outbreaks associated with the HIV virus have made proper diagnosis of TB more difficult. When a person who has TB as well as AIDS is given a TB skin test, the result may not be positive because the AIDS virus kills off the immune-system T cells that produce the allergic reaction needed for test. A chest X-ray may give misleading information, too. More than 50 percent of HIV-infected TB patients have forms of TB that don't affect the lungs. And even when TB *does* affect their lungs, the X-rays look like pneumonia rather than TB.

where they may come in contact with a lot of people—for example, in schools, hospitals, correctional facilities, food-handling establishments, group homes, child-care facilities, and substance abuse centers.

Such requirements are spreading. In New York City, for example, thirty-four cases of active TB were reported in the city jails in January 1988; in January 1991 there were 102 cases in the same prisons.[4] The steep rise prompted New York City authorities to consider plans to screen everyone who is arrested.

Dr. Shalom Hirschman, director of the division of infectious diseases at New York's Mount Sinai Medical Center, points out that thirty years ago people were routinely checked for TB with every new medical examination. Dr. Jack Adler, head of the Tuberculosis Bureau of the New York City Department of Health, recommends that a skin test be done with routine checkups, perhaps every five years. Of course, anyone who has been exposed to somebody with active TB should be tested immediately, and again in six weeks to three months if the first test is negative. And anyone who tests positive should have periodic checkups to make sure the disease does not become active.

Special Testing Situations

Testing over and over for TB will not cause the body to become sensitized to tuberculin and thus cause a reaction the next time. However, a person who has been infected with the TB bacteria may gradually lose sensitivity, particularly after the age of fifty-five. This may result in a negative skin test, even in a person who had been exposed to TB in the past. But the test may stimulate the body to "remember" the TB bacillus, so that if another test is given shortly afterwards it may be positive.

This kind of result can cause confusion. Did the person recently convert from negative to positive (that is, was there a new exposure to TB)? Or did the first test act as a "booster" and help the body remember that it had been exposed before? This booster effect is the reason that when tests are repeated periodically, such as for hospital employees or nursing-home residents, a two-step test is usually conducted. If the initial TB test is negative, a second test is given a week later. If the second test is also negative, the person probably was not exposed to TB. If the second test is positive, then the response probably represents a boosted reaction rather than a recent conversion due to a new infection.[5]

6

Treatment

Soneta was only twenty-three when she came in to the clinic in Philadelphia, but she looked more like eighty. Her arms and legs were so thin they were like sticks, and she stared at the doctor with large, bloodshot eyes. "I been with this cough a month or two now," she said. "Been feeling tired. I don't got no energy. I figured I'd get checked out." She had a 103-degree fever, and her chest X-ray showed white patches over her lungs.

The doctor told Soneta she had TB and explained that she would need to take medications for six months. She was supposed to come in for monthly checkups, but she kept missing her appointments. When she finally came back after three months, she was much worse and complained of "coughing ugly yellow stuff up." Her chest X-ray showed an advanced case of TB. Soneta claimed she had been taking her medicine each day, but after she was admitted to the hospital for intravenous IV antibiotic treatment, she demanded angrily, "What are you doing to me here?" Her urine was bright orange! The color is a normal side-effect of the antibiotic rifampin, and the doctor realized that if Soneta had really been taking her medication she would have been familiar with it. After five months in the hospital, on six different drugs, Soneta finally recovered. Her treatment cost more than $250,000. She was supposed to continue as an outpatient for another six months, but she never came back to the clinic.[1]

Before effective drugs were developed to combat tuberculosis, a person had a fifty-fifty chance of surviving. With drugs, 98 percent of normal TB cases are cured when detected early. However, as drug-resistant strains of TB are becoming more common, the cure rate has decreased. Only half of the multidrug-resistant cases are saved.

Streptomycin, the first antibiotic that was effective against TB, was discovered in 1943–1944 by Selman A. Waksman of Rutgers University in New Brunswick, New Jersey. (He coined the term *antibiotic*.) By 1947 the drug was available for general use. Almost overnight the death rate from TB dropped dramatically. Dr. Waksman received a Nobel Prize for his discovery in 1952.

Streptomycin was used widely, but several problems were encountered. Bacilli developed tolerance to the drug, and the drug produced some damage to the nervous system. To get around these problems, the dosage was lowered, and

TREASURES IN THE DIRT

Selman Waksman first studied the microscopic fungi called *actinomycetes* in a college research project while he was an undergraduate at Rutgers University. He noticed that in the deeper layers of soil, actinomycetes began to outnumber the soil bacteria, and he wondered what the tiny fungi were doing to keep the bacteria from multiplying. Perhaps they were making something that was poisoning the bacteria. Waksman continued his studies of these microbes in graduate school and discovered the species called *Streptomyces griseus* during his master's degree project. Three decades later he happened upon this microbe again, in a culture taken from the throat of a sick chicken. The antibiotic that the culture produced, streptomycin, turned out to be stronger than penicillin, and it worked against tubercle bacilli in guinea pigs. When the drug was tested on a young woman with advanced pulmonary tuberculosis, it cured her—and the first effective TB drug was on its way.[2]

streptomycin was used in combination with another drug, PAS (para-aminosalicylic acid), which had been introduced in 1946 by J. Lehmann of Sweden.

In 1952 isoniazid (isonicotinic acid hydrazide or INH) was added to the list of effective drugs against TB, and the death rate dropped even further. During the 1950s the death rate for children under fifteen dropped 88 percent in the United States and more than 90 percent in Canada, England, and France. INH was used in combination with other TB drugs to prevent resistant bacteria from developing. INH became the most important TB drug.

With these effective drugs, sanatoriums were no longer needed, and many were closed or used for other purposes. Even more effective drugs, such as rifampin, were developed, and doctors believed that tuberculosis was practically cured. Research into the further understanding of tuberculosis was all but stopped as money was spent on other, more urgent health problems.

Early Medical Treatment

Before effective anti-tuberculosis drugs were discovered, treatment for TB consisted mainly of good food, rest, and plenty of sunshine. Early in this century, however, doctors did make use of several medical procedures.

One of the most popular medical practices was *collapse therapy*, which involved collapsing all or part of a diseased lung. This procedure collapsed a cavity inside the lung, allowing the lung to rest and cutting down on the oxygen

Before effective TB drugs were discovered, treatment included fresh air and sunshine, even during the winter months. Here, children from the Preventorium at the National Jewish Hospital in Denver, Colorado play outdoors on a warm winter day in 1929.

available to the bacilli, killing them. One collapse therapy procedure, called *pneumothorax*, was developed in the 1890s by Carlo Forlanini, an Italian physician. Air is pumped into the chest, causing the diseased lung to collapse. In the 1940s more than two-thirds of all TB patients had this type of surgery. In fact, between 1925 and 1950 pneumothorax was performed on 100,000 Americans.[3]

Another procedure, called *thoracoplasty*, was also very popular in the 1930s and 1940s. Ribs were surgically removed to decrease the size of the chest cavity and permanently collapse a lung. The cure rate with this procedure was an amazing 80 percent, but patients were deformed by it and often suffered lung failure years later.

Pulmonary resection or excisional surgery involves removing the parts of the lungs that have been damaged. This procedure was not always effective when it was first developed, but when antibiotics became available to prevent the infection that often followed the operation, it was more successful. When the diseased parts of the lungs have been removed, the remaining healthy parts can function normally. By the 1960s many patients had excisional surgery in addition to medication to make sure a relapse did not occur. This procedure is still sometimes used today in advanced cases.

The most drastic surgical procedures were no longer needed once effective antibiotics were developed and in use. But today, as drug-resistant tuberculosis is becoming more of a problem, doctors are sometimes forced to revert to these older techniques. At the National Jewish Center for

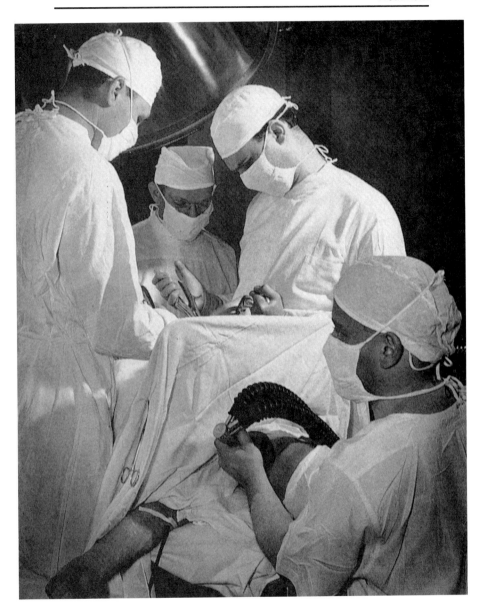

Thoracoplasty, the removal of ribs to decrease the size of the chest cavity, was a treatment used in the 1930s and 1940s. Here, doctors perform the procedure on a TB patient.

Immunology and Respiratory Medicine in Denver, Colorado, where many "impossible" TB cases are now sent, pneumothorax and lung resection are sometimes used as a last-resort alternatives when drug treatment is not working.

Modern Treatment Procedure

What happens when a person finds out he or she has TB? Patients with active TB aren't usually hospitalized. "Usually, they're told to stay home from work for about two to three weeks and take their pills," says Dr. Snider.[4]

Treatment for active tuberculosis includes good nutrition, plenty of rest, and drugs such as streptomycin, isoniazid (INH), ethambutol, rifampin, and pyrazinamide. Several different drugs should be given at once because the bacteria may build up an immunity to one.

Because of the high number of drug-resistant cases in New York City, the New York City health department recommends that its doctors start all patients on four drugs—isoniazid, rifampin, ethambutol, and pyrazinamide—just in case they are drug-resistant. (Remember, it can take up to twelve weeks to find out if a patient has a drug-resistant strain of TB.) If traditional treatment is given, and months later the laboratory results come back indicating the strain was drug-resistant, the patient will have continued to be contagious all that time. In addition, some patients with drug-resistant strains may die before the results come back.

Other doctors are treating all AIDS-related TB cases as if they were drug-resistant, too. "Some think that may be overtreating. The bottom line is, we don't have a good alternative," says Margaret Fischl, AIDS researcher at the University of Miami Medical School.[5]

Most patients are usually not contagious after the first two weeks of treatment, but they have to continue taking a combination of drugs for six months to a year or more. (Drug-resistant cases may require 18 to 24 months and hospitalization.) The treatments take so long because the drugs work by preventing the bacteria from multiplying, then allowing the body's natural defenses to fight the disease.

When a person does not finish all of the prescribed medication, drug-resistant TB may develop. The medicine kills off the most susceptible bacteria, but the more resistant bacteria survive and multiply, and the person becomes sick again. Some patients have been in and out of the hospital time after time because they don't continue taking their medicine. Eventually, drug-resistant strains develop. This is called secondary resistance. But people who catch TB from that person have primary drug resistance, and even if they take their medicine conscientiously, they may not be treatable. The increasing number of primary-resistant cases is making health experts very concerned. A 1991 report found that 23 percent of TB patients being treated for the first time had drug-resistant strains, and 40 percent of the TB bacteria isolated from previously treated patients were resistant to one or more drugs.[6]

Drug-resistant strains have been around for a long time, but in the past they were rare. Now they have been recorded in at least seventeen states. The biggest fear is that unless the new outbreaks can be stopped, there may come a time when the drug-resistant strains replace the treatable ones as the most common form of TB.

Preventive Treatment

"Anybody with a positive skin test is a walking time bomb," as Dr. John Sbarbaro of the University of Colorado puts it, because there is a one in ten chance that active tuberculosis may develop.[7] That is why it's important for everyone to have a TB test at least once in their lives.

What happens when a person has a positive skin test but further testing shows he or she does not have an active case of TB? Anyone who tests positive should have periodic checkups to make sure the disease has not become active. Many people are given the drug isoniazid (INH) in such cases. This therapy is up to 90 percent effective in preventing those with TB infection from developing active TB. (However, doctors are not sure whether this drug on its own will prevent drug-resistant strains from developing.)

The CDC recommends that children and adolescents who have been in close contact with a TB patient should receive INH therapy even if their skin test is negative. After three months they are retested, and if they are still negative the treatment is stopped.

For people over thirty-five, doctors are more cautious about INH preventive therapy because there is a greater risk of suffering side-effects such as liver problems. Those at high risk for TB, such as the HIV-infected and IV drug users, are given the drug and are carefully monitored during treatment to make sure there are no liver problems. "Recent converters" (those who previously had a negative skin test, but then later tested positive, indicating that they recently became infected) and those who have had recent close contact with an active TB case may also be treated, regardless of age, because the risk of developing active disease is highest within the first two years after a primary infection.

INH is usually taken for six months. Those with AIDS may take the drug for twelve months or more, or even for life. Researchers at the University of Medicine and Dentistry of New Jersey (UMDNJ) have found that people infected with HIV who

---

 # WHO SHOULD RECEIVE INH PREVENTIVE THERAPY?

People with a positive skin test who:

- are under 35
- are HIV-infected
- have an abnormal chest X-ray
- have a recent tuberculin skin test conversion
- are recent immigrants from high-risk areas
- are IV drug users
- have medical conditions such as diabetes, silicosis, malignancies, gastrectomy, chronic renal failure, or other illnesses that increase the risk of TB[8]

have a positive TB test live an average of 260 days longer when treated with INH than those who are not treated. HIV-infected people who have a negative TB test live at least two months longer if treated with INH. (Remember that the immune system of AIDS patients may be so damaged that they do not test positive even when infected with the TB bacillus.) The UMDNJ team advises that all HIV-infected people should be treated with INH even before testing them for TB.[9]

Sometimes rifampin is added to the preventive treatment when INH-resistant organisms are suspected. International studies have found that eight weeks of treatment with isoniazid, streptomycin, rifampin, and pyrazinamide may be

SIDE-EFFECTS OF INH

Millions of patients have INH without any problems. But occasionally there are side-effects. The liver may be affected, for example. Symptoms may start with loss of appetite, nausea, and weakness. After about a week the urine may be the color of dark tea or coffee, and the skin and eyeballs will be yellowish. Patients who are at high risk for liver damage should be monitored with frequent liver enzyme tests.

as effective as fifty-two weeks of isoniazid alone.[10] But isoniazid is the preventive treatment currently used in the United States.

A Shortage of TB Drugs?

By the early 1990s U.S. drug manufacturers were no longer making some of the drugs that are used to treat tuberculosis. In our competitive market it is not profitable for drug companies to manufacture drugs that do not have a high demand. TB was not common enough in the United States for drug companies to develop new drugs, or even to continue making old ones. Companies in other countries were manufacturing the drugs, however, because TB has never ceased to be a major worldwide problem.

By the end of 1991 many TB drugs were hard to find, and doctors often had to substitute more costly drugs. Two very useful drugs for treating drug-resistant cases were almost impossible to locate. Ironically, one of them was streptomycin—the first effective TB medication! Streptomycin and para-aminosalicylic acid (PAS) could be helpful in treating drug-resistant cases, but because there were problems with the overseas supplies, they were available only through the CDC. The Food and Drug Administration set out to coax American companies into producing the medication so that they could be used effectively in the United States.

7

TB and Society

Milton Ellison tested positive for TB as a child, and his doctors prescribed preventive treatment with INH. But he never finished the treatment. As an adult he was treated at least three times for active TB, but each time he stopped taking his medication. "It's too many pills, and it's too many pills to take at one time. I can't swallow all those pills," he explained. Ellison, who has been in and out of psychiatric hospitals, homeless shelters, and residential hotels, refused to believe he had tuberculosis because most of the time he didn't feel sick.

Finally, in 1992, health officials detained the homeless man in a hospital, using a 1909 New York State health law that allows a person with a communicable disease to be detained. But Ellison refused to take his pills and spat and shouted at hospital staff members. Finally, he was shackled by wrist and ankle to the bed, and a sheriff's deputy stood guard. After three and a half weeks he was released because he was no longer contagious. Another court order set the condition that he could be released only if he promised to continue taking his medication. His doctors said he would need to take six pills a day for the next four and a half weeks and then twice a week for seven more months. A nurse was going to visit his residential hotel each day to watch him take his medication, but he packed up his belongings and left for New York City, promising he would go to a clinic to get his pills. But he didn't wait for his medication at the clinic the next day because it was overcrowded. Eventually, Ellison entered a hospital for psychiatric treatment, and resumed TB treatment while at the hospital.[1]

Although this is not the typical story of a TB sufferer, it does highlight a growing controversy. Milton Ellison's lawyer claims that health officials violated his civil rights by holding him against his will. Health officials argued that what they did was necessary and that laws need to be made even stronger to make sure patients complete their treatment. Patients who do not complete treatment for TB increase the risk of breeding drug-resistant strains, and in addition to endangering their own lives they endanger many others as well.

The inner-city poor and homeless are one of the biggest populations with TB in this country. But these people are usually more worried about finding food and shelter than they are about getting to treatment centers each day to take their medicine. In addition, there aren't enough centers, and all of

Milton Ellison, shown here, was detained at an Orange County, New York hospital in order to force him to complete his TB treatment.

them are overcrowded. Some patients think it is too much trouble to take so many pills—in some cases, up to ten pills a day. They may no longer feel sick after a few weeks, and they stop going to clinics. Overall, about 40 percent of TB patients in New York City fail to complete treatment.

"The main issue in TB control is getting people to take their medicine," says Dr. Karen Brudney, who studied patients at Harlem Hospital Center over a nine-month period in 1989 and found that 89 percent failed to complete treatment.[2] Of those patients, 27 percent fell sick again within the year.[3]

An Ethical Dilemma

What should society do with people who refuse to be treated? Some doctors believe that the only way to make sure these people take their medication is to confine them. But others believe this is an infringement of the person's rights. In New York City, for example, the American Civil Liberties Union threatened to sue the city for detaining a number of uncooperative patients in city hospitals. The ACLU lawyers are concerned about the patients' rights. But what about the rights of the people who come in contact with them? How important are an individual's rights, compared to the safety of society?

Quarantine Laws

The CDC is reviewing quarantine laws across the country, to figure out a model that all states can use.

In Massachusetts, health officials can detain a person who refuses to complete treatment for a communicable disease for whatever period of time he or she takes to be cured. In the early 1990s a TB treatment unit was opened in a Boston hospital for uncooperative patients. It provides drug treatment and rewards cooperation with privileges, such as day passes.

In Denver, patients who repeatedly don't show up to take their pills at a clinic are locked up in a prison hospital until treatment is complete.

In New York City, more than forty people were detained against their will in the late 1980s and early 1990s. The law in New York was passed back in 1909 to deal with a germ-carrying food preparer who became known as Typhoid Mary. It is rather vague, specifying only that patients can be detained until they are no longer infectious. But then they are free to go. Dr. Jack Adler, medical director of the Bureau of Tuberculosis Control at the New York City Department of Health, looked at the results of thirty detention orders and found that only one or two were cured of TB. "Once they left, most patients went back to being noncompliant with treatment," he says.[4]

The only way to make sure that patients take medication is to use DOT—directly observed therapy—in which someone actually watches a patient take each and every dose of the medication.

Getting People to Complete Treatment

"Tanzania, Malawi, and Mozambique all have 85 percent completion rates," points out Dr. Barry Bloom of Albert

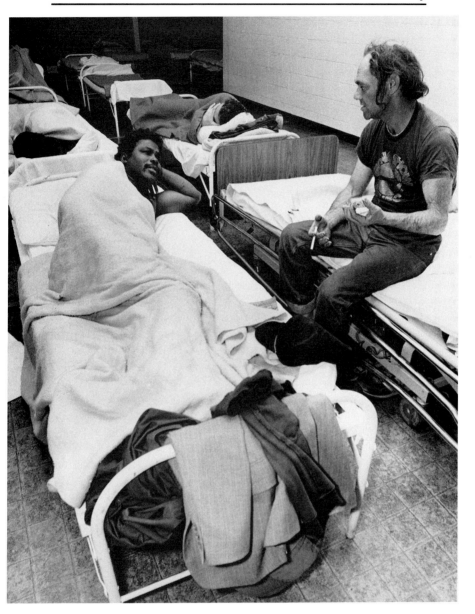

These homeless men, spending the night in a shelter, are at increased risk of contracting TB. The inner-city poor and homeless are one of the biggest populations with TB in the United States.

Einstein Medical College in New York. "Why can't New York City do what a poor country like Tanzania can do?"[5]

Generally, health officials believe that most people who stop treatment need incentives rather than detention. Most TB patients complete treatment when health workers stay in touch with them or coax them to a clinic. But "sometimes it takes a little imagination. Give them a cup of coffee. Talk to them. Pay them an honorarium to come in and take the medicine. If the public doesn't want drug-resistant TB, and if bribing people is the way to get them to take their medicine, then I say bribe them," says Dr. Lee Reichman of the New Jersey Medical School.[6] "We should encourage patients to take their medicine consistently, with accessible clinics,

 # WHO'S NOT TAKING THEIR MEDICINE?

Out of thirty-three patients who were detained in New York hospitals until they were no longer contagious, over a period from 1988 to April 1991, thirty-one stopped taking their medication after they were released. Some died, some got sick again, and some lost contact with the system. More than half of these patients were homeless. Two-thirds had a history of using alcohol, intravenous drugs, or cocaine. Almost half had been hospitalized at least four times for TB, and 73 percent were resistant to one or more antibiotics.[7]

outreach workers, DOT, even an incentive program. There's a range of possibilities from providing a free hot lunch to food coupons or store vouchers, even cold cash. It's cheaper to encourage people to take their medicine than to treat them in hospital when they don't," says New York City's acting health commissioner, Dr. Margaret Hamburg.[8]

Different communities around the world have tried many of these tactics to get patients to complete treatment. In China, village doctors regularly visit TB patients. In Newark, New Jersey, public health nurses bring TB patients coffee and cookies. In Los Angeles, the Homeless TB Patient Incentive Program provides a daily clinic for homeless people. If they take their pills, they receive vouchers for free meals and a room for the night.

Many communities are setting up similar programs to track down TB carriers. In New York City, for example, a group of health workers work full time visiting TB outpatients to make sure they take their medication. Sometimes they have to go searching for patients who have moved or are homeless. Some TB patients resent the interference with their lives. "They'd come here and treat me like a child," complained one woman. But many patients welcome the health workers' attention and cooperate with their efforts. "She's become like a friend," one man said about his caseworker. "When you don't take it you feel like you're stepping on your friend's feet."[9] Health workers also check out relatives of TB patients and test people in drug treatment programs. But as Dr. Adler of New York's Bureau of

A New York City health worker (right) visits with a TB outpatient (left) to make sure he takes his medication.

Tuberculosis Control points out, the funds to keep these programs going are not keeping up with the number of people who need these services.[10]

A Return of TB Sanatoriums?

As public hospitals are filling up with TB patients, many experts believe that sanatoriums should be opened up again. "It's an obvious solution when the indigent TB patient poses direct risk to thousands of others living in shelters," says Dr. Michael Osterholm of the Minnesota Department of Health.[11] Many health experts believe that as the number of TB cases rises, sanatoriums are inevitable.

Fighting TB Around the World

The International Union Against Tuberculosis and Lung Diseases is spending $4 million a year on massive programs for TB detection and control in seven developing countries, including Tanzania, Malawi, Mozambique, and Nicaragua. Each year 65,000 cases are treated, with cure rates of 80 to 85 percent. The World Health Organization, whose Tuberculosis Unit had dwindled to just one health expert in 1989, has now developed a strong new program to conduct TB research and provide technical assistance to developing countries. The World Bank is also contributing to TB control, through substantial loans to China and Bangladesh.[12]

8

Prevention

John, a thirty-four-year-old man from Wisconsin, had been suffering from chronic weight loss, fatigue, night sweats, and a severe cough for about three months before his doctor diagnosed pulmonary tuberculosis.

He was not given a skin test because he had previously had a positive skin test without having the active disease. A chest X-ray was abnormal, and a sputum sample tested positive for acid-fast bacilli. (This is the class of bacteria that includes the tubercle bacillus, as well as a number of others.) A month later the culture was confirmed as *M. tuberculosis*. The drug-susceptibility test results indicated that the bacillus was sensitive to all the normal TB drugs, so isoniazid (INH), rifampin, and pyrazinamide were prescribed.

John's family, friends, and associates were checked out to determine whether they had been affected. Eighteen county and municipal health departments were involved in tracking down 309 contacts.

Among his close contacts, 63 percent were infected. None of his other contacts were infected. All those with a positive reaction had normal chest X-rays, and INH was prescribed for all who were infected. Only one of the close contacts had an active case of TB, and a three-drug regimen was prescribed.

The cost of tracking down and treating this single outbreak was about $15,000. Although John had previously tested positive for TB, he had never been given INH as preventive treatment. If he had, he might not have developed tuberculosis, and he wouldn't have infected forty-five other people.[1]

The most important way to prevent tuberculosis is to keep it from spreading. When poverty exists, the disease can spread because of poor hygiene and nutrition. Improving the standard of living and providing adequate health care for all members of society is more than just a moral issue; it is also a safety precaution to keep diseases like tuberculosis from spreading and becoming a menace to everyone. Of course, this is a rather tall order, and one that no society has been able to fill.

The very least that can be done to keep TB from spreading is to find the people who are suffering from it and cure them as quickly as possible so that they can't spread the disease. One untreated case can cause a dozen others in a year. (More than ten times that total may become infected without developing the disease. Dr. Samuel Dooley, a CDC tuberculosis expert, points out that in one outbreak more than fifty health workers were infected by a single patient.[2])

When a person is diagnosed with TB, close family members, friends, and other contacts should also be checked. According to the CDC, an average of nine contacts are checked for each TB case. Between 20 and 23 percent of those tested are indeed infected with the bacilli.[3] If the patient is very infectious, and several household members are infected, coworkers and other contacts may also be tested. About 1 percent of the patient's contacts are found to have active TB.

Some health experts believe that everyone should be tested for TB so that preventive treatment can be given to those who have been infected. (Remember, one in ten may later develop active TB.)

A Vaccine for TB

The ideal prevention for any contagious disease is to find a vaccine that will help the body build up immunity against the disease so that people will not get it if they are exposed to it. When Robert Koch first discovered the bacterium that causes TB, he tried to find a vaccine that would prevent it. Unfortunately, his vaccine was not effective.

A vaccine called the BCG vaccine (Bacille Calmette-Guérin) was developed by Albert Calmette and Camille Guérin, researchers at the Pasteur Institute in Lille, France, in 1908, and was distributed all over the world by the League of Nations in 1929. It is made from specially weakened tubercle bacilli (*Mycobacterium bovis*), and it is injected into the skin. BCG causes the area where it is injected to react, and then later it may bring immunity against infection. The BCG vaccine is the vaccine most used around the world. More than 2.5 billion people have received it, and it is currently being given to more than 80 percent of the world's children.[4] But it is not used in the United States.

The Vaccine Debate

There are several reasons that BCG vaccine has not been used in the United States. Most experts agree that the vaccine protects children against the deadliest complications of TB, such

JOB HAZARD

Health workers fifty years ago had a different view of the TB hazard, says Dr. Fred Ayvazian, head of pulmonary medicine at a New Jersey Veteran's Administration hospital. Back in the early 1940s, when he was in medical school, it was expected that half a dozen students in each class would get TB. "People weren't frightened as they are today," he says. "It was considered an inconvenience because you went away to the Adirondacks for a few years and graduated a few years late."[5] In fact, some of these recovered TB patients learned so much during their convalescence that they became leading lung specialists. But today, fears of TB are prompting some doctors to switch careers.

as meningitis, but they are not sure how long the protection lasts. Yet in studies of the vaccine conducted on many different groups, its effectiveness has ranged from 0 to 80 percent.[6] One explanation for the contradictory results is that the BCG used in different parts of the world differs in quality. Some researchers have also pointed out that the poorest test results were obtained in areas where infections with other types of mycobacteria are common; people there already have some cross-protection against TB infection, and thus their immunization with the vaccine does not make much difference.

A major drawback of the vaccine is that people who receive it will test positive on skin tests for the rest of their lives. That means that doctors will lose their most reliable way of determining infection with the tubercle bacilli. Today, health care workers are routinely tested for TB. If they were vaccinated, the skin test could not be used to alert them if they became exposed to the mycobacterium. This has been a major argument in the debate on whether health care workers should be given BCG shots.

Dr. John La Montagne, director of the microbiology and infectious disease division at the National Institute of Allergy and Infectious Diseases says, "I am not optimistic that this will be the answer that people think it will be. It won't protect everybody. If it is used, it will be used at a cost: the loss of a very useful screening tool for TB sensitivity. And it may not even protect you."[7]

The vaccine could also have harmful effects for those infected with the HIV virus. That means that health workers would have to undergo HIV testing before they could be given the vaccine. This requirement would only add to the growing controversy about HIV testing and people's right to privacy.

Revamping Hospitals and Prisons

Hospitals and prisons are ideal for spreading the disease because they contain large, vulnerable groups of people, so that every TB case could turn into a crisis. "All it takes to have an outbreak is to have that one patient get into an institutional setting where spread can occur," says Dr. Sam Dooley of the CDC in Atlanta.[8] Yet such institutions can be designed to cope with the problem safely.

Some of the toughest TB cases in the world are sent to the National Jewish Center for Immunology and Respiratory Medicine in Denver. But in nine years only one health care worker has become infected, and no one has developed TB. Patients are treated in properly ventilated isolation rooms equipped with ultraviolet lights to kill TB bacteria. Hospital staff and patients wear tightly fitting masks that keep TB germs out (and cost a mere $1.50).

The National Institute for Occupational Safety and Health recently recommended that health care workers treating TB patients should wear thick rubber masks connected to a motorized air pump, much like the masks worn by scuba divers. Many prominent TB specialists say that such extreme measures are unnecessary and would do more harm than good. Dr. Michael Iseman of National Jewish

93

refers to the devices as "Darth Vadar gizmos." UMDNJ specialist Dr. Lee Reichman points out, "We have to build relationships with sick patients, and if doctors have to get into space suits and wear gas masks, patients aren't going to take their pills. It's probably much more important to teach TB patients to cover their mouths when they cough.[9] He also stresses the importance of isolating infectious cases and making sure that patients take their medicines.

Isolation and proper ventilation systems are especially important for AIDS patients. A CDC report found that drug-resistant strains of TB are spreading in HIV-infected patients because hospitals often do not adequately isolate them from other HIV patients. The CDC recommends that HIV-infected patients with drug-resistant TB should be isolated in rooms with their own ventilation systems[10]

Ideally, *anyone* with an active TB case should be placed in a separately ventilated area until he or she is no longer contagious. Many large facilities are working hard to create or expand isolation areas but, ironically, the areas where the TB rates are the highest are generally served by city hospitals whose funds are most limited.

Hospitals are spending millions to create negative-pressure rooms where air from the room flows out of the building. (This is the opposite of the usual ventilation systems, in which air flows out of the rooms into the hallways.) Exhaust fans, better filters, and ultraviolet lamps to kill TB germs are also being installed. Adequate systems can be created with fairly modest investments. Roosevelt Hospital in New York City,

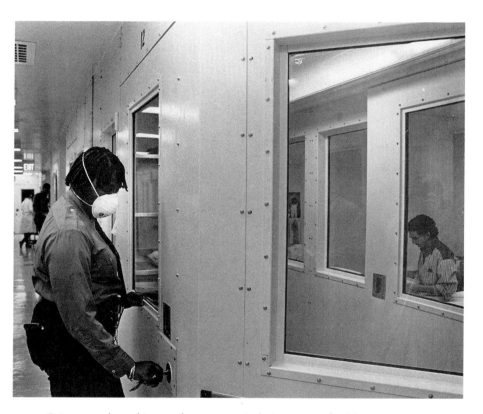

Prisons, such as this one, have set up isolation rooms for TB patients to prevent the spread of the disease.

for example, responded to an outbreak of drug-resistant TB by installing window fans that keep isolation rooms at negative pressure and change the air frequently. The cost was only about $1,000 per room.[11]

Prisons are another source of major concern. "Jails and court pens are places where the disease can rapidly spread and poison the rest of the city," says Robert Gangi, head of the Correctional Association of New York.[12] The situation in New York City highlights this growing problem. In 1992 in New York City about one in five convicts was infected with HIV, and nearly that many tested positive for tuberculosis, but not one jail had separately ventilated cells. In fact, while suspects wait to be charged with offenses, they are crammed into tiny "holding pens" where they may wait—a dozen people in a 10-by-15-foot room—for two or three days before they are sent to jail or back out onto the street.

Efforts are being made to prevent the spread of TB in prisons. New York hopes to begin a screening program for all suspects when they are booked, and in May 1992 a multi-million-dollar, 42-cell, state-of-the-art contagious disease unit was opened on Rikers Island to isolate prisoners with active TB.

9

Tuberculosis and the Future

n 1963 in Dublin, Ireland, Dr. Patrick Brennan was working at trying to figure out how isoniazid kills TB. He gave up on that project a few years later. Early in 1992 Dr. Brennan, now at Colorado State University in Fort Collins, returned to this question and found that no progress had been made in the twenty-seven years since he left it.[1] Later that year, though, a group of researchers announced in the prestigious British journal, *Nature,* that they had determined the chemical structure of the part of the TB bacillus on which isoniazid acts.[2] This was the first time a target of an anti-TB drug had been determined.

New Research Is Needed

Doctors are now faced with the prospect that current treatment might no longer be effective if drug-resistant TB becomes more widespread. No new targets for drug attack on the TB mycobacterium have been discovered in the past twenty years. We need new insights into the life cycle of the tubercle bacillus and how it interacts with the cell that it infects.

Why do we know so little about the world's number-one killer infectious disease when medical research has learned so much about many other diseases? The TB effort has been the victim of its own success. After effective antibiotics were developed, research dollars were taken away from TB and given to other diseases. In 1991 the federal government spent close to a billion dollars on AIDS research, but less than $3 million was spent on TB research. Many researchers left the field, and few were replaced. "We really only have a couple of handfuls of researchers," says Dr. Anthony Fauci, director of the National Institute of Allergy and Infectious Diseases.[3]

Health experts are trying to get new researchers into the field to battle the growing TB problem. "We desperately need new drugs," says Dr. Thomas Daniel, president of the American Lung Association. Dr. Fauci adds, "The pharmaceutical industry will also need to be encouraged to get involved in this problem, since during these years [since the 1950s] they reduced their efforts to develop new or improved therapies for TB . . . . We are fighting TB without new antibiotic therapies and without an effective vaccine."[4] Nonetheless, those researchers already at work are conducting valuable research in several areas.

Many TB researchers conduct their tests using bacteria that resemble that of TB, but grow more quickly and are safer. Shown here are several colonies of similar bacteria, including *Mycobacterium smegmatis.*

How the Body Builds Up Immunity to TB Bacteria

Dr. Ian Orme at Colorado State University in Fort Collins is studying how mice build up immune defenses against TB bacteria. He wears protective clothing, mask, helmet, and gloves, and he sprays TB germs with a large aerolizer to infect the mice in the same way that humans get the disease—through the air.

Dr. Orme has found that the TB mycobacteria live inside the same types of immune cells that the AIDS virus infects—a kind of white blood cell called a helper T or CD4 cell. This may be why people get TB in the early stages of AIDS before the CD4 cells have all been killed.[5] (Another possibility is that the infected T cells are inactivated and unable to mobilize the body's defenses against bacteria.)

Improved Tests

One of the biggest delays in treating tuberculosis properly is that TB tests currently take three to twelve weeks to diagnose the disease. In New York City, the Health Department demanded that hospitals and commercial labs report test results more quickly. Labs are starting to use newer tests, including radiometric and genetic testing, to detect TB faster and to check for drug susceptibility. "Labs are shifting over to the new methods, which will give answers in a day or two, not weeks," says Dr. Thomas Frieden, a CDC expert.[6] Techniques such as the new PCR test may help get patients more specific treatment earlier, and cut down on the time when they spread the disease.

Meanwhile, other researchers are working on imaginative new approaches to TB diagnosis. For example, Dr. William Jacobs, who works with Dr. Barry Bloom at the Albert Einstein College of Medicine in the Bronx, New York, has attached the luciferase gene (which makes fireflies glow) to a virus that infects TB bacteria. If there are TB bacteria in a culture dish, the luciferase will give off a greenish-yellow glow. Using the new test, researchers can diagnose drug-resistant TB in half the time needed for conventional tests.[7]

Solving the Problem of Noncompliance

There are many reasons why people stop taking their medications. They think there are too many of them, and it is too much trouble to wait in long lines at a center to get the medications. But new technological advances will make completing treatment easier. In many parts of the world a single pill that combines three medications can be taken instead of having to take three different pills.

APREX, a California company, has produced a pill bottle with an electronic device in its cap. The cap notes the time and date each time the bottle is opened and can transfer the records to the doctor's computer. Then the doctor can check on whether the TB patient is taking the medications on the right schedule. Improved models with a display to remind patients a pill is overdue are being developed.

Another possibility is a device that is implanted under the

Drug susceptibility testing helps to identify which drug combinations will be most effective for a particular TB patient.

skin and releases medicine directly into the body for a period of time. Researchers at the National Institute of Allergy and Infectious Diseases are exploring this possibility.

The Search for an Effective TB Vaccine

The ultimate goal in wiping out TB is to find an effective vaccine that would prevent the disease from developing. Several researchers are exploring this avenue. New York researchers Barry Bloom and William Jacobs are working on using BCG as a carrier that would piggyback vaccines against many childhood diseases. "There might be a role for BCG here if things get really out of hand," says Dr. Bloom. He hopes to develop a mutant strain of BCG that can't multiply in humans, but that could still immunize them.[8]

Meanwhile, Dr. Jacobs has developed a means of moving genes into and out of TB mycobacteria. Many bacteria can exchange hereditary instructions in the form of small, circular DNA molecules called plasmids. The common intestinal bacteria *E. coli*, which are frequently used in laboratory studies, can do this. No plasmids occur naturally in mycobacteria, but these microbes can be infected by viruses called phages, which also can transfer genetic material from one bacterial cell to another. Dr. Jacobs combined part of a phage that can infect the TB bacillus with part of a plasmid from *E. coli* to produce a hybrid called a phasmid. Researchers can tinker with the phasmid genes while it is in *E. coli* and then use it as a shuttle to carry the changed

FIGHTING DISEASES WITH GENETIC TECHNOLOGY

Genes are found in all living organisms. They are the chemical blueprints that make us who we are. Our genes determine the color of our eyes and hair and the shape of our noses. They also instruct the body to produce enzymes that help the body function. The genes of bacteria contain instructions for their size and shape, what kind of cells they infect, and how deadly they are.

The Human Genome Project, which is attempting to determine the chemical structures of all the human genes, has recently included the TB and leprosy mycobacteria in the program. The complete genetic structure of these bacteria may be revealed within three to five years, say Dr. Bloom and Harvard researcher Dr. Christopher Murray.[9] And with this kind of knowledge, scientists will be able to predict new drug targets and antigens for new vaccines. Using the powerful new tools of biotechnology, researchers can even change a bacterium's genes so that it will no longer cause any harm.

genes into the mycobacterium. With this new tool, scientists can build better vaccines and also study the TB microbe's own genes.[10]

Stopping Drug-resistant TB

In the summer of 1992 European researchers discovered a gene on the tubercle bacillus that may be responsible for some of the drug-resistant strains of TB. The discovery was encouraging to TB researchers around the world. "This is the first time anyone's located anything on the chromosomes that helps control resistance. It's so exciting," says Dr. Joseph H. Bates, professor of medicine at the University of Arkansas, and chief of medicine at the Veterans' Affairs Medical Center in Little Rock.[11]

Scientists are hopeful that this finding may help pave the way for new medicines to treat TB. It could also lead to faster tests that identify drug-resistant strains.

Dr. Stewart Cole of the Pasteur Institute in Paris, working with Dr. Ying Zhang of Hammersmith Hospital in London and their colleagues, found that strains of bacteria that were resistant to isoniazid were missing a gene normally found in tubercle bacilli. When the missing gene was inserted in the organisms, they were no longer resistant to the drug.

The researchers believe the gene probably instructs the bacterium to produce an enzyme that activates the drug. They are not sure yet how the enzyme affects sensitivity to isoniazid, but they believe it may change the drug into a form that is toxic to the bacterium.

"This is the beginning of a very momentous project," says Dr. Michael Iseman of the National Jewish Center for Immunology and Respiratory Medicine, who is an expert on drug-resistant TB. "In the United States and even more in the developing world, resistance to isoniazid has become a major problem."[12] This finding may lead to improved testing for drug resistance. Researchers can design biochemical probes to search for a particular gene. The probes would show within hours whether or not a sputum sample contains drug-resistant strains.

Not all drug-resistant strains, however, are caused by this missing gene. The researchers believe that some strains may have defective genes that cause them to be partially resistant to isoniazid. The missing gene also does not explain resistance to other drugs, such as rifampin. But experts are hopeful about the finding. "It's still so exciting because it's a big first step. With advances like this, tests to detect resistant strains quickly are a reasonable expectation within a few years," says Dr. Bates.[13]

Scientists hope to use this discovery to modify current drugs in order to produce a medication that will be toxic to the drug-resistant strains. If researchers can figure out how the enzyme-activated isoniazid actually kills the organisms, the new genetic insights would allow scientists to design new drugs to kill TB germs. Experts such as Dr. Barry Bloom believe that this finding "offers hope that molecular genetics may be the one way to tackle the emergence of drug-resistant tuberculosis."[14]

Q&A

Q. I thought TB was something people used to get in the old days. Why is it in the news now?

A. By the mid-1980s TB was almost a forgotten disease in the United States. But since 1985 the number of cases has been going up. The growing numbers of HIV-infected people and homeless have provided the conditions for a TB epidemic, and we were slow in responding to the new threat because most of the health care services for TB patients had been closed down. In developing countries, TB never stopped being a major problem; today it is the top infectious-disease killer worldwide.

Q. How do you catch TB?

A. Mainly by breathing in air containing bacteria-carrying droplets coughed or breathed out by people with TB.

Q. Can I catch TB riding on the bus?

A. Maybe, but it's not very likely. Animal studies have shown that as little as one TB bacterium may be enough to cause infection, but usually it takes long, close contact with a TB patient under poorly ventilated conditions.

Q. Is TB fatal?

A. Before antibiotics were developed, many people died of TB. But now it can be completely cured, usually on an outpatient basis. New drug-resistant strains of TB are more difficult to treat, though, especially in people whose immune defenses are already weakened.

Q. I've been coughing a lot lately. Should I get tested for TB?

A. Yes, if you're a student, or you live or work in a place where you come in contact with a lot of people, or if you've been in contact with someone who has TB. In fact, some doctors recommend that everyone should be tested for TB during routine medical checkups. It's much easier to treat TB if it is detected early.

Q. Does a positive skin test mean I have TB?

A. Not necessarily. A positive skin test means you have been exposed to a mycobacterium. More precise tests that take much longer are needed to tell whether it was the tuberculosis mycobacterium. If you have ever received BCG vaccine, you may also have a positive skin test. Even if you have been infected by the TB bacillus, you may not have the disease. TB infection develops into the disease in only about 10 percent of cases. (If a person's immune defenses are damaged, the risk of developing TB is higher.)

Q. Why do some people with a positive skin test get treated with a drug even if they're not sick?

A. Prompt treatment with isoniazid or a combination of drugs can help the body's defenses to kill the TB bacteria and thus prevent an infection from developing into the disease.

Q. If there's a vaccine to prevent TB, why isn't it used in the United States?

A. Studies show that BCG vaccine is not always effective in preventing TB. And once you receive it, you will probably have a positive skin test, so it will be harder to diagnose TB if, later on, you do get the disease.

Q. Why does TB treatment take so long? When I had a strep throat I only had to take penicillin for ten days.

A. The TB bacillus is very well protected from the body's defenses. Antibiotics help to make it more vulnerable, but it takes time to wipe out all the bacteria. If the treatment is stopped too soon, TB bacilli are still alive and may later break out of the tubercles and spread through the body. The germs that survive are more likely to be drug-resistant, and thus much harder to treat.

Q. How can I avoid getting TB?

A. By avoiding crowded, poorly ventilated places. Sensible health measures like taking regular exercise and eating a good diet will also help to keep your immune defenses strong.

TB Timeline

4000 B.C.—Skeletal remains show prehistoric humans had TB.

300s B.C.—Aristotle claimed TB was contagious.

1600s—One out of five people in Europe died from TB.

1679—Franciscus Sylvius described lung nodules as *tubercula.*

1689—Robert Morton used the term *consumption.*

1840—The word *tuberculosis* was first used.

1854—First TB sanatorium was opened.

1865—Jean Antoine Villemin proved TB was contagious.

1882—Robert Koch discovered tubercle bacilli; first TB sanatorium in United States was opened.

1890s—Carlo Forlanini developed surgical procedure called pneumothorax.

1907—Christmas Seals were first used in United States.

1908—BCG vaccine was developed.

1944—Streptomycin, the first effective antibiotic for TB, was discovered.

1952—Isoniazid, one of the most important TB medications, was developed.

1986—Downward trend of TB cases was reversed.

1992—Gene for drug-resistant TB was discovered; target for Isoniazid was determined.

For More Information

American Lung
Association
1740 Broadway
New York, NY 10019
(212) 315-8700

Centers for Disease
Control
Division of Tuberculosis
Elimination
1600 Clifton Road NE
Atlanta, GA 30333
(404) 639-3311

National Jewish Center
for Immunology and
Respiratory Medicine
1400 Jackson Street
Denver, CO 80206
(800) 222-LUNG

New Jersey State
Department of Health
University Plaza
CN 369
Trenton, NJ 08625
(609) 588-7539

New York Lung
Association
432 Park Avenue South
New York, NY 10016
(212) 889-3370

Chapter Notes

Chapter 1

1. Mireya Navarro, "Far Away From the Crowded City, Tuberculosis Cases Increase," *The New York Times,* December 6, 1992, p. L49.

2. Phyllida Brown, "The Return of the Big Killer," *New Scientist,* October 10, 1992, p. 31.

3. Reuters, "America Fighting a Rematch with 'Beaten' TB," *The Star-Ledger* (Newark, N.J.), May 24, 1992, p. 16.

4. David Levine, "A Killer Returns," *American Health,* April, 1992, p. 9.

5. Barry R. Bloom and Christopher J. L. Murray, "Tuberculosis: Commentary on a Reemergent Killer," *Science,* August 21, 1992, p. 1056.

6. Richard Stone, "Tuberculosis Rebounds While Funding Lags," *Science,* February 28, 1992, p. 1064.

7. Janice Hopkins Tanne, "The Truth About TB," *New York,* November 5, 1990, p. 92.

8. Laurie Garrett, "What You Should Know," *New York Newsday,* March 8, 1992, p. 37.

Chapter 2

1. William H. Allen, "The Great White Plague: A History of TB," in *The World Book Health & Medical Annual, 1990,* p. 141.

2. Ibid.

3. René and Jean Dubos, *The White Plague* (New Brunswick, N.J.: Rutgers University Press, 1952), p. 6.

4. Ibid.

5. Allen, p. 141.

6. Ibid., p. 143.

7. Evelyn Zamula, "Tuberculosis: Still Striking After All These Years," *FDA Consumer,* March 1991, p. 21.

113

8. Lawrence K. Altman, "Tuberculosis Medicine Conquers an Ancient Disease", *The New York Times,* March 30, 1982, p. C3.

9. Allen, p. 142.

10. Zamula, p. 18.

11. Kathleen Doyle, "Stamping Out Tuberculosis," *American History Illustrated,* November/December, 1989, p. 68.

12. Ricki Lewis, "The Prescription Drugs and Human Health," in *The World Book Health & Medical Annual, 1990,* p. 368.

13. David Levine, "A Killer Returns," *American Health,* April, 1992, pp. 9–10.

14. Lawrence K. Altman, "Deadly Strain of Tuberculosis Is Spreading Fast, U.S. Finds," *The New York Times,* January 24, 1992, p. B1.

15. Mary Benanti, "Doctors Preparing to Fight U.S. Tuberculosis Outbreak," *The Courier News,* April 28, 1992, p. A1.

Chapter 3

1. Phyllida Brown, "The Return of the Big Killer," *New Scientist,* October 10, 1992, p. 31.

2. Lawrence K. Altman, "Deadly Strain of Tuberculosos Is Spreading Fast, U.S. Finds," *The New York Times,* January 24, 1992, p. B1.

3. Phyllida Brown, "TB Returns to Haunt America," *New Scientist,* November 9, 1991, p. 13.

4. Bethany Kandel and Mary Smaragdis, "Tuberculosis Raging in Many Cities," *The Courier News,* August 14, 1991, p. A7.

5. Geoffrey Cowley, "A Deadly Return," *Newsweek,* March 16, 1992, p. 53.

6. Woodard, "TB in NY," p. 37.

7. Cowley, p. 55.

8. Catherine Woodard, "Ancient Enemy of Man Returns," *New York Newsday,* March 9, 1992, p. 4.

9. Woodard, "TB in NY" p. 36.

10. Lawrence K. Altman, "Top Scientist Warns Tuberculosis Could Become Major Threat," *The New York Times,* February 11, 1992, p. C3; Laurie Garrett, "Tackling the TB Puzzle," *New York Newsday,* March 12, 1992, p. 115.

11. Laurie Garrett and Catherine Woodard, "The Risk in Hospitals," *New York Newsday,* March 10, 1992, p. 6.

12. Janice Hopkins Tanne, "Q & A About TB," *New York,* March 23, 1992, p. 31.

13. "Hospital Staffs' Risk of TB May Be High," *Medical Tribune,* June 11, 1992, p. 6.

14. Cowley, p. 56.

15. Garrett and Woodard, p. 6.

16. Tanne, p. 31.

17. Bethany Kandel and Mary Smaragdis, "Tuberculosis Raging in Many Cities," *The Courier News,* August 14, 1991, p. A7; "Atlanta Plans Fight Against Disease Surge," *Medical Tribune,* June 11, 1992, p. 6.

18. Tanne, p. 32.

19. Cowley, p. 54.

20. Mary Benanti, "Tuberculosis Spreads Among Minorities," *The Courier News,* April 3, 1992, p. A6.

Chapter 4

1. D. J. Schoetz, Jr., "Case Record 44–1991," *The New England Journal of Medicine,* October 31, 1991, pp. 1295–1302.

2. Laurie Garrett, "What You Should Know," *New York Newsday,* March 8, 1992, p. 5.

3. Janice Hopkins Tanne, "The Truth About TB," *New York,* November 5, 1990, p. 92.

4. Ibid.

5. Ibid, p. 31.

6. Ibid.

7. Ibid, p. 92.

8. Geoffrey Cowley, "A Deadly Return," *Newsweek,* March 16, 1992, p. 54.

9. Evelyn Zamula, "Tuberculosis: Still Striking After All These Years," *FDA Consumer,* March 1991, p. 20.

10. Tanne, 1990, p. 93.

11. Cowley, p. 54.

12. Catherine Woodard, "TB in NY," *New York Newsday,* March 8, 1992, p. 36.

Chapter 5

1. Gurney Williams III, "Health Alert! A Deadly Disease Returns," *Family Circle,* January 12, 1993, p. 42.

2. Janice Hopkins Tanne, "The Truth About TB," *New York,* November 5, 1990, p. 93.

3. Evelyn Zamula, "Tuberculosis: Still Striking After All These Years," *FDA Consumer,* March 1991, p. 22.

4. James Barron, "Panel Recommended Ways to Fight TB in New York Jails," *The New York Times,* June 25, 1992, p. B5.

5. Patrick T. Dowling, "Return of Tuberculosis," *American Family Physician,* February, 1991, p. 463.

Chapter 6

1. Neil Skolnik, "A Breathing Lesson," *Philadelphia,* July 1991, pp. 39–45.

2. Marguerite Smolen, "A Nobel Quest," *Rutgers Magazine,* Winter 1992, pp. 43–45.

3. Mary Ann Fitzharris, *A Place To Heal: The History of National Jewish Center for Immunology and Respiratory Medicine* (Denver, Col.: National Jewish Center, 1989), p. 47.

4. Janice Hopkins Tanne, "The Truth About TB," *New York,* November 5, 1990, p. 95.

5. Geoffrey Cowley, "A Deadly Return," *Newsweek,* March 16, 1992, p. 57.

6. Barry R. Bloom and Christopher J. L. Murray, "Tuberculosis: Commentary on a Reemergent Killer," *Science,* August 21, 1992, p. 1061.

7. Tanne, p. 94.

8. *TB Fact Sheet: Including Information on TB and HIV,* 1990 Centers for Disease Control fact sheet.

9. Joan Whitlow, "Jersey Researchers See Hope in Anti-TB Drug," *The Star-Ledger* (Newark, N.J.), June 12, 1991, p. 5.

10. Patrick T. Dowling, "Return of Tuberculosis," *American Family Physician,* February, 1991, p. 466.

Chapter 7

1. Mireya Navarro, "Recalcitrant Patients a Threat as TB Returns," *The New York Times,* April 14, 1992, pp. A1, B2.

2. Lisa Belkin, "TB Threat: Not Taking the Medicine," *The New York Times,* November 18, 1991, p. B1.

3. Geoffrey Cowley, "A Deadly Return," *Newsweek,* March 16, 1992, p. 56.

4. Janice Hopkins Tanne, "Q & A About TB," *New York,* March 23, 1992, p. 35.

5. Geoffrey Cowley, "A Deadly Return," *Newsweek,* March 16, 1992, p. 56.

6. Ibid, p. 57.

7. "HIV Positives Prone To Mycobacteria Infections," *Medical Tribune,* June 11, 1992, p. 6.

8. Tanne, p. 35.

9. Mireya Navarro, "Pill Monitors Make Sure TB Patients Swallow," *The New York Times,* September 5, 1992, p. 1.

10. Dina Van Pelt, "TB Resurgence Plagues Officials," *Insight,* February 25, 1991, p. 54.

11. Cowley, p. 57.

12. Barry R. Bloom and Christopher J. L. Murray, "Tuberculosis: Commentary on a Reemergent Killer," *Science,* August 21, 1992, p. 1061.

Chapter 8

1. CDC Newsletter *TB Notes,* Winter/Spring 1992, p. 7.

2. Lawrence K. Altman, "Deadly Strain of Tuberculosis Is Spreading Fast, U. S. Finds," *The New York Times,* January 24, 1992, p. B1.

3. Janice Hopkins Tanne, "The Truth About TB," *New York,* November 5, 1990, p. 95.

4. Lawrence K. Altman, "Stymied by Resurgence of TB,Doctors Reconsider a Decades-Old Vaccine," *The New York Times,* October 15, 1992, p. B4.

5. Elisabeth Rosenthal, "TB, Easily Transmitted, Adds a Peril to Medicine," *The New York Times,* October 13, 1992, p. B2.

6. "BCG Vaccine Considered," *Medical Tribune,* June 11, 1992, p. 6.

7. Ibid.

8. Catherine Woodard, "TB in NY," *New York Newsday,* March 8, 1992, p. 4.

9. Rosenthal, p. B2.

10. "TB in Hospital Linked to Ventilation," *Medical Tribune,* June 25, 1992, p. 6.

11. Rosenthal, p. B2.

12. Mitch Gelman, "A Prison Breeding Ground," *New York Newsday,* March 11, 1992, p. 23.

Chapter 9

1. Laurie Garrett, "Tackling the TB Puzzle," *New York Newsday,* March 12, 1992, p. 115.

2. Barry R. Bloom and Christopher J. L. Murray, "Tuberculosis: Commentary on a Reemergent Killer," *Science,* August 21, 1992, p. 1061.

3. Garrett, p. 115.

4. Mary Benanti, "Doctors Preparing to Fight U.S. Tuberculosis Outbreak," *The Courier News,* April 28, 1992, p. A1.

5. Garrett, p. 115.

6. Janice Hopkins Tanne, "Q & A About TB," *New York,* March 23, 1992, p. 34.

7. Garrett, p. 115; Elyse Tanouye, "Gene That Gives Fireflies Their Glow May Light the Way for TB Treatments," *The Wall Street Journal,* May 7, 1993, p. B6.

8. Tanne, p. 34.

9. Bloom and Murray, p. 1058.

10. Mark Caldwell, "Resurrection of a Killer," *Discover,* December, 1992, p. 64.

11. Elisabeth Rosenthal, "Scientists Identify What Is Making TB Resistant to Drugs," *The New York Times,* August 13, 1992, p. A1, D19.

12. Ibid, p. D19.

13. Ibid.

14. Emily T. Smith, ed., "One Step Toward Stopping the New Tuberculosis," *Business Week,* August 24, 1992, p. 77.

Glossary

AIDS (acquired immune deficiency syndrome)—A disease in which the body's disease-fighting cells are damaged or destroyed.

alveolus (pl. alveoli)—A tiny air-filled cavity in the lungs.

BCG vaccine—A weakened form of *Mycobacterium bovis* used in most of the world to provide protection against tuberculosis.

compliance—Cooperation of patients in taking medications and following instructions to complete their treatment.

contagious—Able to be transmitted from one person to another.

DOT (directly observed therapy)—Public health practice of requiring patients to take medications under observation by a health worker.

drug resistance—Ability of a disease microbe to survive and multiply in the presence of a drug that would ordinarily kill or disable it.

false negative—A test result showing the absence of infection when it is actually present.

false positive—A test result apparently indicating the presence of infection but actually due to some other cause.

hemoptysis—Coughing up blood.

HIV (human immunodeficiency virus)—The virus that causes AIDS.

immunity—The ability to resist a disease through the action of disease-fighting cells adapted to attack an invading microbe or its products.

infection—The presence of harmful microbes in the body. Infection may not cause symptoms of disease if the body's defenses can hold it in check.

isoniazid (INH)—An antibiotic drug used against tuberculosis.

macrophages—Disease-fighting cells that can engulf and digest microbes.

Mantoux test—A test for TB in which purified tuberculin extract is injected under the skin; swelling indicates a positive test.

meningitis—Inflammation of the meninges, the membranes covering the brain or spinal cord.

miliary tuberculosis—A rare form of TB in which small nodules are formed throughout the body.

mycobacterium—A group of bacteria including *Mycobacterium tuberculosis* (the tubercle bacillus), which causes pulmonary TB in humans, and *M. bovis*, which infects cows and humans and causes TB in bones and joints.

negative-pressure room—A room ventilated so that air flows into it when a door or window is opened.

pneumothorax—An operation in which air is pumped into the chest, causing a lung to collapse.

pulmonary tuberculosis—TB that affects the lungs.

relapse—A recurrence of symptoms of disease after apparent recovery.

sanatorium—A health facility for rest, treatment, and rehabilitation of people with chronic diseases.

smear test—Microscopic observation of sputum samples treated with chemicals.

T cells—Types of white blood cells (lymphocytes) involved in defense against disease.

tine test—A TB test in which purified tuberculin is applied to the skin with a multipronged puncture device.

tubercle—A small, hard swelling in which invading TB microbes are walled up.

tuberculin—A liquid extracted from the tubercle bacillus.

vaccine—A preparation of microbes or their products given in a vaccination to stimulate protective immunity against disease.

Further Reading

Allen, William H. "The Great White Plague: A History of TB." *The World Book Health & Medical Annual, 1990*, pp. 141–152.

Altman, Lawrence K. "Deadly Strain of Tuberculosis Is Spreading Fast, U.S. Finds." *The New York Times*, January 24, 1992, p. B1.

———."Drug-Resistant TB Makes U.S. Rethink Elimination Program." *The New York Times*, January 28, 1992, p. C3.

———."Stymied by Resurgence of TB, Doctors Reconsider a Decades-Old Vaccine." *The New York Times*, October 15, 1992, p. B4.

American Lung Association. "Facts About Tuberculosis." 1991 brochure.

———."Pills to Prevent TB." 1985 brochure.

Bloom, Barry R., and Christopher J. L. Murray. "Tuberculosis: Commentary on a Reemergent Killer." *Science*, August 21, 1992, pp. 1055–1063.

Brown, Phyllida. "The Return of the Big Killer." *New Scientist*, October 10, 1992, pp. 30–37.

Caldwell, Mark. "Resurrection of a Killer." *Discover*, December, 1992, pp. 59–64.

Centers for Disease Control. "A Strategic Plan for the Elimination of Tuberculosis in the United States." *Morbidity & Mortality Weekly Report* (Supplement), April 21, 1989.

———."TB Fact Sheet: Including Information on TB and HIV." CDC fact sheet.

Cowley, Geoffrey. "A Deadly Return." *Newsweek*, March 16, 1992, pp. 53–57.

Davidson, Paul T., George Diferdinando, Lee Reichman, and Dixie Snider. "TB: Coming Soon to Your Town?" *Patient Care*, May 15, 1992, pp. 40–66.

Doyle, Kathleen. "Stamping Out Tuberculosis." *American History Illustrated,* November/December, 1989, pp. 66–68.

Dubos, René, and Jean Dubos. *The White Plague: Tuberculosis, Man and Society.* New Brunswick, N.J.: Rutgers University Press, 1952, 1987.

Fitzharris, Mary Ann. *A Place to Heal: The History of National Jewish Center for Immunology and Respiratory Medicine.* Denver, Col.: National Jewish Center, 1989.

Levine, David. "A Killer Returns." *American Health,* April, 1992, pp. 9–10.

———."Rising Death Toll from Tuberculosis Is Alarming Health Experts." *American Health,* April 1992, pp. 9–10.

Lueck, Thomas J. "After 2 Cases of TB, Commodities Trading Floor to Require Employee Tests." *The New York Times,* July 23, 1992, p. B3.

Mahmoudi, Artin, and Michael D. Iseman. "TB: The Captain of All These Men of Death Returns." *Britannica Medical & Health Annual,* 1993, pp. 241–245.

National Jewish Center for Immunology and Respiratory Medicine. "Tuberculosis." Med Facts fact sheet.

Navarro, Mireya. "Far Away from the Crowded City, Tuberculosis Cases Increase." *The New York Times,* December 6, 1992, p. L40.

———."Pill Monitors Make Sure TB Patients Swallow." *The New York Times,* September 5, 1992, pp. 1, 22.

———."Recalcitrant Patients a Threat as TB Returns." *The New York Times,* April 14, 1992, pp. A1, B2.

Nunn, Paul. "Tuberculosis: The HIV Connection." *New Scientist,* October 24, 1992, pp. 41–42.

Rosenthal, Elisabeth. "Doctors and Patients Are Pushed to Their Limits by Grim New TB." *The New York Times,* October 12, 1992, pp. A1, B2.

———."Drug-Resistant TB Is Seen Spreading Within Hospitals." *The New York Times,* August 1, 1992, pp. 1, 9.

————."Scientists Identify What Is Making TB Resistant to Drugs." *The New York Times*, August 13, 1992, p. A1.

————."TB, Easily Transmitted, Adds a Peril to Medicine." *The New York Times*, October 13, 1992, pp. A1, B2.

Smolen, Marguerite. "A Nobel Quest." *Rutgers Magazine*, Winter 1992, pp. 43–45.

Specter, Michael. "Neglected for Years, TB Is Back." *The New York Times*, October 11, 1992, pp. 1, 44.

————."Tougher Measures to Fight TB Urged by New York Panel.," *The New York Times*, November 30, 1992, pp. A1, B2.

Tanne, Janice Hopkins. "Q & A About TB." *New York*, March 23, 1992, pp. 30–35.

————."The Truth About TB." *New York*, November 5, 1990, pp. 92–95.

Van Pelt, Dina. "TB Resurgence Plagues Officials." *Insight*, February 25, 1991, p. 54.

Voelker, Rebecca. "The Lengthening Shadow of Tuberculosis." *The World Book Health & Medical Annual 1993*, pp. 55–67.

Woodard, Catherine. "TB in NY." *New York Newsday*, March 8, 1992, pp. 4–5, 36–37.

Zamula, Evelyn. "Tuberculosis: Still Striking After All These Years." *FDA Consumer*, March 1991, pp. 18–23.

Index

lymph system, 44

M

macrophages, 42, *43*, 44, 47, 121
Mantoux test, 57, 58, *121*
meningitis, 45, 92, 121
Miami, 32
miliary tuberculosis, 44–45, 121
milk, 36, 39
Molière, 12
Morton, Robert, 110
mucus, 40, 41, 47
Murray, Christopher, 104
mycobacteria, 36, 104, 121
Mycobacterium avium, 38
Mycobacterium bovis, 36, *37*, 39,
    91, 121
Mycobacterium leprae, 38
Mycobacterium smegmatis, *99*
Mycobacterium tuberculosis, 36, 61,
    88, 121

N

National Association for the Study
    and Prevention of
    Tuberculosis (NASPT), 20
National Jewish Center for
    Immunology and Respiratory
    Medicine, *18*, *69*, 70, *71*, 72,
    93, 106
negative-pressure rooms, 94, 121
Newark, New Jersey, 31, 85
New York City, 29, 31, 32, 33, 72,
    81, 82, 85
noncompliance, 66, 73, 78, 81,
    82, 84, 101, 103
nursing homes, 28, 29, 31
nutrition, 72

O

old tuberculin (OT), 57
Orme, Ian, 100
Osterholm, Michael, 87

P

para-aminosalicylic acid (PAS), 5,
    68, 77
patient rights, 79, 81
PCR (polymerase chain reaction)
    61, 100
phasmid, 103
phlegm, 59
phthisis, 12
plasmids, 103
pneumothorax, 70, 121
polymerase chain reaction (PCR)
    61, 100
"post-primary" tuberculosis, 41,
    45–47
prevention, 5, 88–96, 109
primary infection, 42, 44
"primary" TB, 41
prisons, 28, 29, 31, 63, 93, *95*, 96
pulmonary resection, 70
pulmonary tuberculosis, 44,
    47–49, 121
purified protein derivative (PPD),
    57, *58*
pyrazinamide, 72, 76

Q

quarantine, 81–82

R

Raucher, Beth, 25
reactivation, 41
Reichman, Lee, 49, 50, 84, 94
relapse, 54, 121
research, 97–106